Personal Growth and Development

# HEALING ANIMALS WITH REIKI

## MONIQUE JOINER SIEDLAK

Oshun
Publications

**Cover Design by MJS**

Cover Image by adogslifephoto@depositphotos.com

**Published by Oshun Publications**

www.oshunpublications.com

# Contents

# Other Books in the Series

Want to learn about African Magic, Wicca, or even Reiki while cleaning your home, exercising, or driving to work? I know it's tough these days to simply find the time to relax and curl up with a good book. This is why I'm delighted to share that I have books available in audiobook format.

Best of all, you can get the audiobook version of this book or any other book by me for free as part of a 30-day Audible trial.

Members get free audiobooks every month and exclusive discounts. It's an excellent way to explore and determine if audiobook learning works for you.

If you're not satisfied, you can cancel anytime within the

trial period. You won't be charged, and you can still keep your book. To choose your free audiobook, visit:

**www.mojosiedlak.com/free-audiobooks**

# WANT TO BE FIRST TO KNOW?!

# JOIN MY NEWSLETTER!
MOJOSIEDLAK.COM/SELF-HELP-AND-YOGA-
NEWSLETTER

# Introduction

Humans and animals do not operate on the same level of consciousness or subconsciousness. Animals work on a more spiritual field where they sense things in a more energy-matter way. This is why so many of us depend on our furry companions as a way to heal ourselves or feel better when we are upset. Reiki healing is a type of energy that involves all universal life force. Basically, Reiki a way we can grasp hold of our own energy then draw from the universe and use the intent of this energy for healing and compassion for our animals.

Originating in the late 1800s in Japan, Reiki has been practiced and experienced by many people across the globe. Reiki is used not only on people but animals too. Its effects are beneficial to all because of the non-invasive practice it offers. The transfer of this energy can be done through long-distance, in-person hands-on, or at a distance but hovering over a subject's body. You will learn that Reiki focuses mainly on balancing the energy points in an animal's body by pinpointing the pain or imbalance in the Chakras in our bodies.

In this book, you will learn the powerful effects Reiki

healing has on your own individuality, on your personal spirit, on the environment, and on loved ones around you. You will also learn how to implement Reiki into your meditative practices so that you can practice this flow of energy transfer with your own pets. Reiki benefits all animals in all sizes and helps quicken the healing process for pain and injury. It helps heal and relax the mind, so that past trauma is more comfortable to cope with. While it also eases aggression and helps diminish behavioral problems in animals that are instinctively hyper or high maintenance.

Do you want to help your animals as they help you? Do you want to learn how to communicate with them on a different level? Have you imagined a life where you and your pets can finally be on the same page? By understanding Reiki and the use of its natural healing through your personal energy, you can ultimately help your animals.

Enjoy the experience of Reiki. Discover how to master the technique of communication with your pet and bring it to another level.

## ONE

## What is Reiki Healing

IN THE LATE 1800s, A TYPE OF ENERGY HEALING CAME TO society's knowledge in Japan called Reiki. It is stated to be a transfer of universal energy from the practitioner's hands to their patient. In Japan, Reiki means universal life energy: Rei, universal; and Ki, life energy (Newman, 2017). You may be wondering what people talk about when they refer to a person's energy or aura. Primarily Reiki manifests from our own personal energy points (five points of energy) and is the transfer of our intent onto our object–person or animal. Have you ever been extremely upset about something and your best friend comes to give you a hug that makes you feel a little better? Or maybe you have had a bad day and seek the comfort of your spouse to cuddle with. After that, your mood heightens, and you feel a little better. These are two examples of taking and transferring energy onto someone else as a way to feel better. Before we dive any further into Reiki energy, we are going to take a closer look at our own personal energy and where it comes from. Once we officially get in tune with it, we can further understand the transfer of it onto something (animals or people), which is what Reiki is mainly about.

Everyone retains internal personal energy in five different

ways. One way is physical, which you can see in the form of weight, shape, and volume. Then we have etheric, emotional, mental, and spiritual. The last of the four forms you cannot see very well, because they are based on a feeling of vibrations rather than a physical sense. The five points of energy make up the human energy field. We need to fully understand and tap into before we can figure out how to grasp Reiki and use it to heal. Our internal energy may be in balance or out of balance. If it is out of balance, it can promote physical and mental problems such as chronic pain and chronic stress. Someone with spiritual abilities is a person who can see and implement the second, third, fourth, and fifth energy points. For example, someone with clairvoyance abilities can sense someone's aura just by touching, smelling, or even hearing them. So, let's look deeper into what each individual energy point is:

## Physical Energy

Our physical energy is the foundation that holds all other energy points. You can view physical energy as our physical beings. It's flesh, bone, organs, and blood, which are the fundamentals of our physical energies. The difference between the physical energy from the other four energies is that we can actually see, touch, and smell this energy sense.

## Etheric Energy

If you have ever heard of an aura, then this is essentially what the etheric energy is. You cannot see it or touch it unless you are a professional energy practitioner, but you can feel it and sense it. Our etheric energy is located around us about half an inch outside of our bodies. Think of it as our own personal bubble. This is why upon first meeting someone you have a sense of the individual—whether they are friendly, safe, comfortable, or not any of these traits. Professional practitioners refer to the etheric energy as the blueprint or holographic form of the physical body, which feels sticky like a spider web or stretchy. Most auras or etheric energies come in color blue, gray, or a grayish blue tinge.

## Emotional Energy

The third point of energy is our emotional sense. This is the point in which our feelings and fears reside and can be quite unstable when it is unbalanced or extremely high.

## Mental Energy

Our mental energy is where our thoughts, values, and belief systems reside. It's the area of energy where we learn how to perceive things and acknowledge personal truths. Everything we experience and learn; we draw from our mental energy. Then we choose to release our knowledge through actions or invisible vibrations.

## Spiritual Energy

The spiritual form of our energy is where we draw our energy from. It's the place where our subconscious, consciousness, and greater awareness reside. Spiritual energy is the universal energy used in almost all other practices, including Wiccan, Chakra Healing, and Reiki Healing. It connects us to our past lives and our universal awareness within ourselves but also to a higher power.

For those of you who understand things on a more scientific level, I will use emotional and mental energy as my next example. Our emotions stem from our thoughts and vice versa, which primarily comes from our mental energy point. Having that said, it is our feelings and thoughts are created based on our experiences, which are formed in the hippocampus center of our brains. The hippocampus, associated primarily with memory, sends signals to the amygdala. These thoughts are brought on by our experiences. Once our experiences are filed into feelings and emotions, the amygdala sends these files to the hypothalamus center of the brain.

The hypothalamus is responsible for sending hormones to the physical parts of our bodies. When we feel fear, the hypothalamus sends cortisol hormones to our body to help us fight the perceived threat or run from it. When we feel happy or euphoric, the hypothalamus sends hormones like endorphins and serotonin to enhance our feelings of happiness. These three parts of the brain are known as the limbic system. They come together in the limbic system to help us experience surroundings, think about our thoughts, and feel our emotions.

When we talk about internal energy points, such as emotional and mental energy, they come from the same place in our brains–the limbic system. Reiki is about tapping into our energy points and then transferring our positive emotions (or healing energy) onto someone else through our spiritual energy points.

With your animals, have you ever sensed something was wrong with no apparent signs that anything was wrong? With people, you can almost sense a tension in the room. If you have ever walked into a room and everyone goes silent, you get the feeling that people just finished talking about you. This is a universal emotional and mental energy that we sponge up in a sense, to allow us to deal with the circumstances we are experiencing at the moment.

Some individuals like to refer to it as intuition or emotional intelligence. Be that as it may, just because someone is emotionally intelligent doesn't necessarily mean you will feel better after talking to them. People who experience a high-energy sense are those who are clairvoyant. They are open to all matter that makes up our universe, and they are connected to their higher selves.

Reiki is a type of energy healing. This means a Reiki practitioner would apply one of their personal energy points to heal or balance your energy as a sense of healing your mind, physical wellness, or spiritual awareness. On account of this, you may feel less chronic pain. More in tune with yourself and be able to control your emotions better if you have some sort of mental illness such as anxiety or depression. If your energy were to be unbalanced, this would cause emotional pain, chronic physical pain, or the inability to be empathetic.

So, energy healing (Reiki) basically targets these energy fields and detects if there is a blockage, and then the practitioner will draw out this negative energy and fundamentally heal you.

Why do people try to open up their Reiki healing powers? What is it used for? Here are some findings about the uses of Reiki, so that you can understand the real power of healing your animal when you tap into your personal Reiki healing.

- The immediate effect of a Reiki session is to relieve stress and tension. It's the practice of learning how to relax muscles. To decrease any emotional and mental pressure of everyday life.
- It reduces pain and stiffness. The relief can be felt within minutes of a Reiki session.
- Reiki diminishes mental blockages resulting in self-love and acceptance.
- It helps bring inner peace to our mind and soul so that we can make wiser decisions. Reiki teaches us gratitude and forgiveness, so we don't hold hate in our hearts or minds.
- Reiki opens our mind to promote intelligence so that we perceive things with more clarity.

- It helps strengthen and rebuild love and acceptance with our loved one.
- Reiki promotes understanding between individuals, even if the opposing party isn't aware of your Reiki healing session.
- It furthers success if the Reiki energy is applied to a future event such as birthdays, birth, fertility, marriage, graduation, etc.
- Reiki promotes positivity within an individual and re-establishes physical, mental, emotional, and professional well-being.

Reiki can cleanse, heal, and rejuvenate in a spiritual sense, enhancing the physical and mental wellbeing of an individual. It purifies our thoughts, words, and actions so that we can take advantage of all life forces that surround us. Essentially, Reiki is the act of transferring positive energy onto another as the sole intent behind the action to heal and promote success and happiness.

TWO

What Is Animal Reiki
_____

MANY PEOPLE MISTAKE REIKI AS SOMETHING YOU DO. BUT Reiki isn't something you do; it's something you learn with the intent of helping others. It's not a tool to fix problems and rid one from disease or physical pain. Reiki is aid through your own energy points to help heal animals and people alike. Along with the many benefits Reiki has on people, it also has the same benefits on animals–if not more.

Reiki promotes relaxation, relieves stress and tension, and provides comfort for the practice of healing the animal being practiced on. A lot of people take advantage or seem not to notice what animals go through because they are so busy and concentrated on their own lives. Animals, just like us, go through challenging moments, become overly stressed or depressed, and can develop physical and mental diseases.

The reason why so many people may turn to Reiki healing or try to do it themselves is that Reiki healing can be done hands-on, hands-off, or from far distances. Each method has the same effects and outcomes. Mostly, instead of developing and gaining your own energy, it's the transfer and firm belief that your animal will become well again. You are focusing all your absolute empathy and beliefs into your own mind, through your body, following this energy subconsciously, and then transferring it from your palms and into the animal itself.

When practicing this, you must master Reiki meditation on your own time and fully understand the system of Reiki (both of which will be explained in the following chapters). You must be fully in tune with your own abilities and awareness so that you can tap into your intuition. Once achieved, you will be able to practice Reiki the right way, and you know that it is being done correctly.

For example, Reiki scanning is known to find the cause of the illness or the problem. Reiki scanning is known as intuitive medical scans. Substantially, you are scanning the animal for any issues by taking in their energy to figure out what the initial problem is through your intuitive skills and awareness.

Most animals are susceptible to this type of energy healing technique because they possess healing abilities themselves. For example, a child with special needs or a veteran will have a service animal. Typically, this will be a dog, to help them with their PTSD or physical disabilities, perhaps fetching pills for their human. Cats and other animals hold the label emotional support animals because they release specific vibrations when they sense that you are distressed or upset.

Think of Reiki as a way to give back to our fur babies for healing us in the same we can treat them. Reiki is very safe for all animals. It is a very gentle approach as you can do it from different parts of the world, away from your animals. This is especially helpful for animals that aren't fond of strangers. It also works for skittish animals since you don't necessarily need to touch them to deliver benefits. The advantage of having a practitioner do Reiki healing out of your home is that your animal is in their element and already relaxed. If your animal is not relaxed or comfortable, the Reiki healing will not work to its full potential.

Reiki is an automatic positive approach because the focus behind it is to heal through love and affection. It does not depend on any sort of belief technique that can lead to harm. Animals perform well to energy healing because they instinctively live in the moment and have no preconceived opinions to overcome. Simply put, when they are stressed, they're stressed. When they are in pain, they're in pain.

If you are still having a difficult time understanding how Reiki works, think of it like this. It's kind of like quantum physics in the thought that everything is made up of matter. That matter is made up of energy. This suggests that everything is connected somehow in some way. We know that we get cell service or WIFI wirelessly. In this sense, it is precisely like long-distance Reiki healing. All energy travels through a wireless (invisible) connection through vibrations.

Everything on this planet reacts to us through vibrations. The plants, earth, air, people, animals, wood, dust, food, etc. The Reiki practitioner will tap into their subject's frequency, which means they are tapping into the energy force that surrounds them (animals included). Once the practitioner's energy connects to their subject's frequency of vibrations from their energy, the session can begin. The practitioner transfers their feelings of love and compassion (personal emotional energy point) to heal their patients. The participant or subject (animal or human) will sense feelings of tingling sensations or a stronger amount of heat in some regions of their body. Then comes a sense of calmness and relaxation wherein the patient is now at peace.

## The Difference Between Reiki and Animal Reiki

The benefits of using Reiki Healing are not restricted to humans. The Reiki that is given to humans is precisely the same Reiki that is provided to creatures. The Universe has all types of animals that can go through from sickness, anxiety, and grief. While we decide to apply the energy given by the Universe, animals are not very fortuitous.

Humans can support other humans with Reiki healing through sending levels of energy to another if they are willingly accepting. Their systems are constructed to obtain communications of the mind that deal with emotions and discomfort. Animals only experience that they hurt and that they are doomed to experience.

Meditation is the primary distinction in human and animal Reiki healing. You have to discover that relationship that makes an animal feel loved and cared for.

Animals are exceedingly perceptive to energy. They can feel an array of emotions like stress, grief, worry, and suffering. Through Reiki healing, you can move inside of a pet or animal and build an understanding of compassion and kindness. They will perceive this as a link. Once this individuality has been created, you can settle and soothe whatever ails a pet or animal through a metaphysical bond and trust.

Connecting with pets can be a sympathetic means of displaying to them how much more satisfying their ways of life can be. These animals may not see the interpretation behind the movement, but it brings positive outcomes just the same.

## Benefits of Reiki Healing

Reiki healing is so difficult to explain or simplify. If you are not a practitioner or have done it or witnessed it at least once, you can never truly understand the full potential that Reiki holds.

Basically, your animals are there to support, comfort, and ease your pain, while also reducing significant amounts of stress. With Reiki, it allows you to do the same for them through the transfer of your energy, closeness, and love. The benefits that come from a single Reiki session, whether long-distance or close to home, are endless. Through this chapter, you will see it is pretty straightforward to understand what an animal can experience through the practice of Reiki.

The reason it works so well and is potentially frowned upon by doctors or veterinarians is that it is not scientifically proven to work and in a sense. Reiki relies entirely on the transfer of energy. However, Reiki has been shown to work on many animals as well as humans. It balances the physical, emotional, mental, and spiritual aspects of the patient by releasing any blockages. Any type of energy block can create the overload of emotional baggage, or overwhelming mental illness, and the exhausting effects from physical pain.

Through Reiki scanning, you can figure out the root cause of your pet's condition that is making it distressed or otherwise acting atypically. The cool thing about Reiki is that your animal gets to decide how much energy they want to take or can take from you or a Reiki healer and for exactly how long. This way, you don't have to guess or wear yourself down with the transfer. With that said, keep note that Reiki should not be a replacement for veterinarian medical care, but seen instead as an aid in the diagnosis to recovery.

Furthermore, here are some proven benefits showing how the practice of Reiki works:

- Promotes healing after a severe surgery or illness
- Increases bonding and trust between owner and pet
- Provides pain relief when medication needs to be taken or before having to go to the vet
- Balances the energy of not just the practitioner, but for the animal too, thus releasing energy blockages
- Increases relaxation, much like a sedative, which reduces stress and tension in the muscles
- Generally, reduces feelings of distress and anxiety
- Helps with separation anxiety or change, such as a big move or plane ride
- Strengthens the immune system
- Provides comfort to upset animals

- Decreases behavioral issues
- Increases the bond shared between pet and owner beyond the initial foundational bond that comes with ownership
- Enhances overall well-being

It's safe to say that with these known benefits in mind, it is worth giving Reiki a try on your pet, no matter which stage of sickness they are in. For example, they could be completely healthy, but you merely would like to strengthen your bond together. Reiki can help bring you closer, especially after time apart.

Since Reiki is such a gentle and non-invasive practice, the animal will feel special, loved, and well cared for, which initially creates a respectful and well-mannered pet. With this close bond, a sick or dying pet may want to stick around longer than they can because of the shared energy created by the relationship resulting in more pain and emotional distress.

Reiki can help the owner and the pet let go and alleviate this type of distress so that it is easier to pass on. Due to Reiki's ability to strengthen the immune system, pets that have developed a kind of cancer. They may need chemotherapy or radiation, and Reiki healing will feel more relaxed when they need to get this type of therapy. The stress of these treatments for cancer can be so debilitating already. With Reiki used as a calming technique, the animal will not feel much pain or sickness due to the effect and benefits Reiki offers.

Are you ready to know more about Reiki and all that you can do to develop it, obtain it, and use it? Get ready to find out how in the rest of this book.

THREE

## Does Reiki Have Side Effects?

WHEN IT COMES TO ALTERNATIVE MEDICINE, REIKI IS ONE OF the most popular forms of therapeutic healing that is intended for helping bolster the healing abilities of the patient to cure all types of sicknesses. Even though there are usually no side effects that involved with Reiki, there are some practitioners which warn patients that part of the healing process might actually mean a detoxifying cleanse which may bring about some type of unpleasant after-effects. Although the side effects are not common, there is a possibility of this occurring.

### Cleaning

After Reiki therapy, practitioners claim that the patient's body would very hard to heal itself. The fact is that the body might try to accomplish the healing by cleaning its tissues and organs of toxins. When this happens, it is cautioned that the patient might experience specific side effects such as headaches, diarrhea, or indigestion, which would only last a day or two after the treatment. On the other hand, many practitioners claim that Reiki is a non-intrusive method of healing and that it has no side effects whatsoever, besides the possibility of the patients feeling calm and relaxed after the procedure which is why they might feel sleepy.

## Attunements

Patients that undergo the Reiki attunement are cautioned as they might experience a cleaning period that ranges from a week to up to three weeks of duration. During the attunement procedure, the healer would open the chakras of the patient to provide him or her with the ability to receive the energy by oneself or herself, without having the need of the Reiki practitioner to do so. It is during this time that the body would detoxify itself of the toxins which had been built up over time. Feelings and thoughts would also be released, which are no longer useful to the health of the patient.

## Criticism

Some wellness experts and practitioners point out that another possible side effect of undergoing Reiki is that the patient might develop a sort of psychological dependency on their Reiki healer, despite the fact there has not been any scientific evidence to prove this. Many people say that such a claim is indeed a scam which has been perpetrated by hoaxers. There have been various researches on Reiki to prove that Reiki is an effective form of treatment for any condition.

FOUR

## The System of Reiki

THE SYSTEM OF REIKI CONSISTS OF HEART, HEAVEN, AND EARTH energy. At the same time, according to Japanese Buddhist and creator of Reiki Healing, Mikao Usui, we are all guided by an invisible life force, which is personal energy.

This hidden life force controls our physical, mental, and emotional well-being. Usui states that energy blockages come from negative thinking, post-traumatic experiences, and stress overload. When this happens, we function at a less than ideal level rather than if we were positive, healed, and distressed.

Reiki allows us to perform at a level where our energy flows freely. Many people who have been through a Reiki healing session describe the experience as calming, grounding, and enlightening. Others say that their experience felt more like an emotional realignment.

Think of it as seeing a chiropractor. Instead of realigning your bones and muscle tension, you are realigning your emotional energy to create a balance so that you can live happily. The same effects happen to animals through an animal Reiki healing session.

Some practitioners in Reiki train for years to understand the energy and how to navigate subtle energy shifts within themselves and in their participants. However, the process of Reiki is something anyone can learn and something you can learn fairly quickly.

## Step One: Receiving Energy

With any Reiki practice at the start, you must activate or tap into the energy within yourself first and foremost. To do this, go somewhere quiet, get comfortable, and close your eyes. Then take a couple deep breaths from your stomach (push your stomach out as you inhale and purse your lips on the exhale). Visualize a white light flowing out of the top of your head internally to your heart, and then follow this light out through your arms and palms. Silently or out loud ask for the points in yourself where you most need healing. This is so important because if you were to try to heal someone else or an animal through Reiki, you wouldn't be giving them your blocked energy. This ensures that the process works to its full potential.

After asking to be healed where you need it most (mind, thoughts, emotions, physical pain, etc.), you should feel a constant flow of energy. Take this in and embrace its full effect as you continue to breathe mindfully. If you notice that you are distracted or your mind starts to drift, accept that this took place, and come back to your breath. Visualize your body as a vessel for healing. Then set your internal intention to its utmost positivity and pray for guidance on receiving healing to your higher power.

## Step Two: Reiki for Sleep

Now that you have learned to receive healing and tap into your own energy points within yourself, you can start to help others. This first step needs to be done every single time, as there might be some extra baggage you were unaware of. If you are giving this healing session to a family member or friend who has difficulty with sleeping, get them to lie down. Position yourself near the top of their head and imagine a steady stream of healing light rush from your hands transferring to the back of their head. This helps them clear their mind of and pain or uncomfortable feelings and emotions experienced throughout the day or weeks.

The next step is to request your participant to take several (approximately seven to ten) deep belly breaths while you slowly count. Count three to five seconds on the inhale, and five to seven seconds on the exhale. Next, ask your participant to visualize their whole day one detail at a time. Ask them to be grateful or to thank each memory before letting go and moving onto the next one (out loud or silently). Let them know that when they are ready to move onto the next event of the day, to let it go on their exhale. All the while, you should still continue to count for them.

By this time, they should be drifting off to sleep as you continue to transfer your energy through your hands slightly above their head. The logic behind this working is that you are sending them your own personal white light of energy healing into their entire body. To escalate or grow your intentions, imagine their body becoming healed, at peace, and heavy as they drift deeper into their sleep. When you notice that they are completely asleep, continue your practice for another fifteen to thirty minutes to give them the full feeling of peacefulness.

## Step Three: Reiki for Stress

Cortisol and adrenaline hormones play a big part in us feeling anxious or afraid. These hormones are why you get symptoms that manifest as the fight-or-flight response. When someone feels stressed, the fight-or-flight syndrome might take effect and can make someone hyperventilate automatically.

In Reiki healing for stress, after you have followed step one, your focus should be mainly on the participant's shoulders. The point is to channel energy down through their shoulders into their whole body. You are going to want to make them stand or sit comfortably while placing your hands on their shoulder for ten to fifteen minutes. Focus on your healing light and on sending it from their shoulders down through their whole body. Ask them to breathe deeply with you as you take slow deep breaths yourself.

Naturally, this will bring up the intense stress they are holding hidden away. If your participant prefers to lie down through this process, you can easily place your hands behind their heads as well.

Wait for at least twenty minutes before ending the session. This is to give the participants enough time to relax and feel the effects of their tension, stress, or anxiety lifting away.

## Step Four - Final Step: Sealing Off Energy

This step is mainly about gratitude. When ending a session, take some time to cleanse, re-heal, give thanks and close your energy. To start, simply shake your hands to eliminate any negative energy, and cup them close in front of you in a position similar to a praying mantis. Speaking out loud or in your head, say thank you to yourself, the energy you transferred, and the participant for their openness.

Keep this in mind that while you are doing these sessions. With an adult, kid, pet, or another animal, adults may not feel much of a difference at first. They have become less aware of their energy points and their physical body. Regardless, just because they didn't feel anything, it doesn't mean that the session didn't work. Some effects take longer than others to show. Kids, on the other hand, are more receptive to gaining, and transferring energy; so keep them in the know about what you are doing. Encourage them to practice themselves, so that they can be experts at energy healing and healing themselves in the future.

Now we will move on to the actual system of Reiki. Essentially, it is a set of Japanese group practices that when used and combined together, can create spiritual growth and healing support. Basically, these group practices are seen as the five elements that make up the Reiki system:

- Reiki precepts
- Hands-on healing
- Reiju and attunements
- Meditations and methods
- Symbols and mantras

The Reiki system is based on learning and understanding more about the hara, which in Japanese means belly, abdomen, or stomach. The hara is the main focus in which is considered to be our body's ultimate source of energy stimulation. Basically, saying that energy comes from and circulates in this part of the body – from there it expands. However, there are actually two other points in the body that energy can regulate. One is the head, the other is the heart.

Although the hara or the abdomen is Reiki's primary focus for where to produce and release energy, these other two points combined with the hara are called the three diamonds. When all three of these places in the body are connected successfully, it creates wholeness and balance within oneself. The reason the hara, or abdomen, is the principal energy healing focus is because it is the first to be developed, balanced, and healed. It is the body's central axis point.

This is where Earth, Heavenly, and Heart energy stem from. The Earth energy is the hara, heavenly energy being the spiritual focal point, and the heart energy is your emotions. In Buddhism, the diamond represents an analogy of self. Diamonds on a more physical sense can cut through almost anything humanity attaches it to. So, in a metaphorical sense, the diamonds of Earth Ki, Heavenly Ki, and Heart Ki bring back the actual substance of life as seen in the reflection of the diamond.

## Earth Energy

Earth energy (the hara) in Reiki healing means that we use our universe and our environments as tools for healing and grounding. This basically means that in earth energy or within your abdomen, wherein earth energy forms, you store your original energy. Simply put, earth energy is the type of energy you were born into this world with. The hara is the energy that connects you or grounds you between yourself and universal life forces (all that surrounds you).

Since Earth energy is the energetic basis of the triangle of the Reiki system, it is safe to say that this part of the system must always be balanced and healed. Earth energy is the foundation that holds all of the other energies in place. It keeps everything tied together. Think of Earth energy as something that is built up in the metaphorical analogy of making a stew. You start with water, Earth energy, and then you add spices, vegetables, broth, oil, etc. into your soup. Simply put, the other experiences in life added to the Earth energy to build upon). The practitioner (you) needs this foundational energy to develop anything else outside of it.

Earth energy offers a powerful grounding healing technique, which provides both mental and physical strength. When someone is grounded, they feel confident, self-worthy, secure, stable, safe, and linked as one to their environment. By working on Earth energy, your base that supports the other diamonds. You subsequently develop concentration, patience, and strengthen your mind as well as letting the Earth energy support the different systematic energies revolving around Reiki.

## Heavenly Energy

Heavenly energy or spirit energy connects you to your intuition or psychic abilities. It is in these abilities where you may see colors and auras. This type of energy is essential for you to keep balanced so that you will be able to see anything beyond just the immediate. The immediate is this physical world. Maintaining balanced heavenly energy means that you will be able to listen to your intuition. Read why, how, and where a person or pet needs the most healing; and be able to get the guidance you need from your higher self to be able to heal successfully.

This Heavenly energy that one develops is known as expansive energy. It makes practitioners such as you more intuitive and bright-minded. Aside from Heavenly energy being strictly spiritual, it is associated with the mind, brain, or head area. It aids you in your efforts to find your spiritual connection while you practice stillness within your mind and self. This means that you will work on being one with yourself. Approaching your inner-critic or negative thoughts through your awareness abilities to better hear what your inner guide is telling you. When this area of energy is balanced and improved, visions and colors become vivid to the human eye.

When working through the system of Reiki, it is best to start at the base energy. Remember, is Earth. Then working to balance and develop its polar opposite, that being the Heavenly energy. When you do this, you avoid and prevent problematic imbalances that affect your health.

Let's say someone is working on their Heavenly energy while skipping or dismissing their Earth energy. What would happen? Their grounding, although they would be able to help many other people through healing, would never be able to help themselves truly. Whether intentional or not, today's society makes us feel as though we must tap into our spiritual side (Heavenly energy) first. Even before ever learning about what our Earth energy is about. Without the base of our energy working and healed, we are incapable of solving root issues within ourselves. We will never experience our fullest potential for feeling maximum growth.

## Heart Energy

The emotions you experience, both empathetically and personally, are what connect you to your heart energy. In this center, you learn your life's purpose and what you were created or put here to do and become. In other words, the heart energy is everything that you have experienced from childhood to adulthood and back again. Simply put, when you were a child, you were without much life experience. As you grow into the adult you are becoming, you draw from each lesson in your life, making you that same child except with more experience. The heart energy is centered not just by your emotions but also by your inner-child.

The third and last diamond, which is the Heart Ki, is developed and created when you successfully learn how to balance and merge Earth Ki and Heavenly Ki. Symbolically, the Heart Ki is centered and can be felt in the center of your chest. When this energy gets tapped into, someone can experience radiating light and warmth from all different directions. In this light, negative feelings such as fear, stress, resentment, pain, etc., are all resolved, which promotes positive emotions such as love, peace, kindness, forgiveness, and so on. A successful balance of the Heart Ki is when both body and mind are healed and at inner peace. When this process is complete, to feel one with yourself internally and externally, small problems and petty details don't matter. Your mind has opened up to the bigger picture—your full potential. Energy is no longer wasted on fear, worry, or tension.

Just as the diamond must come to a close, the Heart Ki is what closes it. To be at a complete balance with your Heart energy in Reiki, you must first master the balance of your body and mind (Earth Ki and Heavenly Ki). Mostly it's when you finally return to the official state of your well-being and return to the heart of things.

When it comes to Reiki healing, in all honesty, regardless of the system, Reiki is about learning one thing. To find complete inner peace with yourself to have the capability to heal yourself, so that you can treat others. When you look outside the box, true emotional healing is about self-worth, respect, and acceptance.

To implement and grow, Reiki healing on a person's and animal's (mainly animals), you must have the ability to heal your inner being truly. This is done through Earth Ki so that you can get to the step of Heart Ki. Without that ability to be aware of all three diamonds of the Reiki healing system, it may be challenging to give healing to your pets and animals.

In the next chapter, you will learn about the meditation practice of Reiki. Before you can fully experience ways to heal and help your pets through the love and kindness you give to them by first giving it to yourself.

When you think of Reiki healing for your pets and other people's animals, think about the energy transfer from yourself to them. It's as if in a way you take their pain away. Perhaps, the most helpful way you can do this is by understanding the healing methods your animals have on you and other people. In this sense, to develop and experience Reiki healing in the most positive way, you should have an empathetic mindset. Imagine yourself at your worst and darkest moments where all you want to do is push everything and everyone away.

Your pet, whether it is a cat, dog, bird, hamster, horse, pig, or cow, absorbs your emotions. They do this, in the same manner, our children do because they both have one thing in common. They don't have any predetermined thoughts or expectations, as they are susceptible to all types of energy that flow through our universe at a continuous rate.

Now that you have thoroughly learned about and understand Reiki, we can move onto the next chapter, which you will learn how to meditate. You will learn to meditate not just for yourself but for someone else too. Mastering this is what it takes to be a true master in healing by your natural Reiki senses.

## FIVE

## Reiki Meditation

AT THE BEGINNING OF THE PREVIOUS CHAPTER, YOU LEARNED how to receive Reiki energy from within yourself to set the process of healing others in motion, including yourself, other people, and animals. Through this process, you may have noticed I asked you to be aware of your distractions and wandering thoughts. Then you were asked to bring your attention back to the present moment and focus on the light, to bring you back to what you were doing. This is called mindfulness meditation. Before we jump into what Reiki meditation is, the things you can do to develop and improve your awareness around Reiki healing, we should learn about meditation altogether. When you have the full picture, you will be able to understand Reiki meditation more easily.

So, what exactly is meditation? Think of it as a way of training your mind rather than your body. It is a practice in which we focus our awareness on our breath to center our thoughts and be aware of what happens in our body. Different meditation techniques are used, along with Reiki meditation. These different types are all used for different things. For example, there is a meditation practice to help you become aware of your thoughts to improve your mindset. There is another meditation to help you become confident and love yourself. There is also mindfulness, which you can do anywhere, at any given point in time. Also, there is meditation to bring you back to your breath. This is used as a distressing technique along with transcendental meditation, a type of meditation used solely to bring your awareness to your spirituality.

What these meditation practices have in common is that they all include you being aware of and bringing your focus to your breath at the very beginning of each exercise.

Regardless of the benefits of this collection of meditation practices, two meditations stand out first. You should practice these two before you dive into other meditative techniques, such as Reiki meditation. These two essential meditation practices are concentration meditation and mindfulness.

**Concentration meditation** is bringing your entire focus to one object, for example, a flame, a spot on the roof, or a rock on the ground.

**Mindfulness** is a type of practice that allows you to watch yourself and what you do in the given moment you are in. This includes your thoughts, physical bodily feelings, emotions, and anything that you are doing.

For example, if you are drinking tea or doing the dishes, your sole focus would be on that warm cup in your hands, noticing the taste, smell, feel, etc. Another example is perhaps when you are grabbing one dish at a time, intentionally washing it and being entirely in the present moment with that one dish.

These two meditative practices strengthen your concentration and awareness abilities. When you do practice Reiki healing, you are already in tune with yourself as well as being completely focused on your healing subject. When you first start meditating, you may discover that you have a limited attention span wherein your thoughts may continuously wander. This is part of the process because essentially you are training your brain to refocus. With practice, this wandering thought process will decrease, and you will get better and better towards mastering meditation techniques.

We learned the benefits of Reiki, but what are the benefits of meditation?

- Better mental and physical health
- A healthier resting heart rate
- Less generalized anxiety symptoms and feelings
- Increase in awareness of oneself and the surroundings
- A constant sense of inner peace

Aside from these benefits of just meditating, some people experienced with meditation also go on to try yoga. Yoga is a physical workout that also encourages learning to meditate during the exercise. Yoga has many health benefits and can allow you to open up your mind for different possibilities in your life. The purpose of meditation is not to simply reap its many benefits, but to also achieve a deeper understanding of oneself. This is essentially the foundation of a Reiki healing practice.

Reiki meditation does not require just center exclusively on Reiki healing practices. It is used for many things, including cleansing the soul, creating internal peace, and finding a Chakra based focus. Whichever Reiki meditation you focus on, they will both be used in two ways: 1) to clear your mind, or 2) to bring your focus to a particular subject. The main difference between Reiki meditation and other meditations is that Reiki teaches you and allows you to bring your attention to your own personal energy points. This is explained earlier.

As Reiki is the transfer of universal energy that encompasses all elements of life, it is the action brought on by the intent behind your work. For example, when you are working on an animal or pet to heal their burdens, your intention should be solely focused on the animal and the work of treating them. Primarily, by definition, Reiki energy flows through all things that connect us to the universe.

Tapping into this is what Reiki meditation allows us to do. In the meditation practice to develop your Reiki senses you basically concentrate your focus on all the energy points within yourself and what the Earth and your environments provide you. Its purpose is to draw from the universal energy to deeply understand your healing potential. As you become attuned to your personal energy through Reiki meditation, you can feel connected to pure Reiki energy–the universal life force. When someone masters the art of Reiki meditation, they can truly create a sense of tranquility and peace in their mind, body, and soul.

## Reiki Zen Meditation

Zen Reiki meditation is the exact same as any Reiki healing meditation or practice, except with one difference: the increased focus of intention.

**Before You Start**

Find a place to sit down where you won't be disturbed by noise or traffic. You can also lie down for this practice. Close your eyes and relax your body.

**Preparation**

Sit or lie there while your eyes are closed and purposely draw in a deep breath. Make sure you are breathing through your nose and out through your mouth. Allow all the air to fill your stomach and all the air to release from your lungs. Do this until you feel completely relaxed and your mind has become hushed.

**Relaxation**

Now, bring your attention to your internal body. Find where your energy lies. Is it your gut (Earth Ki), Chest (Heart

Ki), or Head (Heavenly Ki)? Once you find your energy, feel the flow of it. Let it run through every inch of your inner being. Imagine it running through your veins and your blood traveling within you everywhere.

### Energize

Once you have spotted your energy, felt the flow of it, and then you can embrace it. This is the energizing part of the practice because you can allow yourself to continue to explore this as long as you want.

Zen meditation is solely about observing the flow of your energy without doing anything. You don't have to change the direction, you don't have to heal any part of yourself or rid negativity. Just sit, focus on the energy flow, and embrace it, then it will, as a result, energize you.

### Reiki Cleansing

This meditation in Reiki is used to clean and flush out negativity and toxins from your soul or someone else's. It's meant to rid the non-beneficial energy from you and embrace the positive, beneficial energy within you.

### Before You Start

Lie down or sit comfortably in a calm atmosphere, one where you will not be disturbed. Relax all of your muscles and take one deep breath in. Release it, then close your eyes if they aren't closed already and turn your mindset towards healing and cleansing your body and mind.

### Preparation

Take a deep breath in, pushing your belly out and hold it. Imagine happiness, kindness, and positivity flowing into your body with this breath. As you exhale, release all the baggage or negativity that you have been holding. Remember to take your time and exhale slowly until the stress and negativity are gone. Repeat this process until all is gone, and you feel relaxed and at peace.

### Relaxation

The more you repeat the previous step, the more relaxed

you should feel. Hold the intent of what you are doing behind every breath. Say to yourself: I am breathing in good luck and happiness, I am breathing out negativity and anger. You may notice the more you repeat this mantra with your full intent behind the breaths and the words, the more you will become deeply relaxed. Eventually falling into a state of self-cleansing.

**Energize**

Notice without judging yourself or the thoughts that come into your mind. The distinctive part of the energizing step is that by the end of the session, you should feel at ease with yourself. You should also feel as though a weight has been lifted. You should feel energized to the point of pure peaceful-ness and as though you are a feather. This is because you just sent your tension and stress away with the pure intent that positivity would take its place.

Reiki cleansing is about ridding your mind and body of the tension and stresses that have built up from the day or previous weeks. When you do this, it will be easier to develop and improve healing techniques, especially when you want to use animals as your clients. Cleansing works to clear your body of the negativity. You do not need to pass this onto your matter unintentionally.

## Center Finger Method

The founder of Reiki, Mikao Usui, taught this method to improve concentration during all Reiki meditations or healing practices.

**Before You Start**

Sit, lie down, or stand anywhere you would like. The place you go to do this concentration method is up to where you feel most comfortable, but it is preferred that it happens in an area with no other distractions. When you are ready, place your hands together with each part touching their opposing hand's parts (fingers to fingers, palms to palms).

**Preparation**

Close your eyes and find where your energy is placed or resting within your body. As you get better at Reiki healing, your energy should always spread throughout your body. Bring your focus to this energy and then imagine the energy coming all at once to your middle fingers. Keep this energy focus on the middle fingers during the whole process.

**Relaxation**

There is no relaxation part of this exercise as it is more about awareness and intentionally bringing your energy to where you want it. Some people say they feel more relaxed after the process.

**Energize**

Stay in the hand-to-hand position until you feel that all your energy has reached to JUST your middle fingers. When you notice your attention span focusing on other things, recognize this, and re-center your focus. Press just your middle fingers together to bring your attention back to what you are doing. Refocus, and do this until you do not become distracted for some time.

The point of this exercise is to train your brain to stay focused. To concentrate on the moment at the given task. It works for future circumstances as you master this method because once your mind starts to wander in a Reiki healing session, the focus becomes broken. In that case, you must restart the healing process. This method is also for being able to point your energy to where you need it for however long you need it before you release it. It is used explicitly for Reiki healing.

## Chakra Reiki Meditation

Chakra meditation is a necessary method because Reiki is closely associated with all seven Chakras. The seven Chakras are:

- **Crown Chakra** – Top of the head (Heavenly Ki), the ability to connect to your spirituality
- **Third Eye Chakra** – Between the eyes on your forehead, to see the bigger picture
- **Throat Chakra** – Located within the throat, balancing your communication effectiveness
- **Heart Chakra** – Above the heart in the chest (Heart Ki), empathic abilities and the ability to love fully
- **Solar Plexus Chakra** – Upper belly area, to be confident and in control of our lives and our situations
- **Sacral Chakra** – Two inches below the navel, lower abdomen (Earth Ki), the ability to accept our experiences and each other
- **Root Chakra** – Base of the tailbone where the spine meets buttocks, helps to aid in grounding

Every one of these seven Chakras holds a specific meaning and color. They represent personal health and life for an individual. They are the energy in our body that is connected to each organ that the human body obtains. Reiki and Chakra are similar in the aspect of when something is blocked. For example, if a Chakra is blocked, so is our organ or life energy connected to it. If our diamond points are blocked (Earth, Heart, and Heavenly Ki), then we are blocked energetically, physically, and mentally. Typically this means our ability to Reiki heal may be blocked as well. Moving forward, here is the process of Chakra meditation for Reiki:

**Before You Start**

Move yourself to a couch, bed, or a place where you can comfortably lie down in a quiet environment. To start, take in a deep breath and exhale as you usually do to make your brain aware that the meditation is beginning.

**Preparation**

Once you are ready and calm, close your eyes and focus your attention on the lowest Chakra, the Root Chakra. Visualize that part of your body while also focusing your attention on the energy that flows within that point. When you feel that this Chakra is sufficiently stimulated, you can choose to heal it or keep it stimulated. Then, move your focus to the next Chakra, the Sacral Chakra. Repeat these steps with the Sacral Chakra until finished and then move on to the next one, and so forth.

**Relaxation**

Relaxation in this process only begins once you have finished with one Chakra and moved onto the next. A full Chakra relaxation will present itself to you once the steps of all Chakras is complete with healing or stimulation.

**Energize**

Once all Chakras are stimulated, you will feel a release of your body as it lets go of all tension or blockages. After there are no blockages in your spirit, the energy you recognize will be lifted. You are at full strength to be able to heal and do what you wish. Meaning, there will be a better chance you succeed at healing other people and animals through Reiki.

This type of meditation is crucial to master. It helps you feel completely in tune with your own energy through Reiki and with the Chakra points. A way to feel more at peace and energetically aligned.

## The 21-Day Reiki Meditation

The twenty-one day Reiki meditation helps you take the time to develop focus, spirituality, and complete goals and visions. It consists of three weeks, and through each week, you will have completed something new, awakening your spirituality deeper and deeper within yourself.

**Week One**

The first step is to create your intention or ask a question.

In front of you draw the Usui symbol - hands held in prayer palms and fingers pressed together and then focused your base energy to your solar plexus (Earth Ki). As you inhale deeply, imagine that you are the symbol's essence. When you slowly exhale through pursed lips, allow this energy to take over every cell of your body. Allow it to move through your body into your mental, emotional, and physical body. Once you have succeeded in doing this, ask your question, or focus your intent.

Sit with this energy and intent or question for up to 20 minutes. If you find that you have lost focus, reinstate the symbol with your hands three times and re-visualize the energy coming from your palms into the rest of your body and mind. When this process is complete, end your session and throughout your day, imagine the light of Reiki with you in all your moments.

Do this every day and keep a journal so you can record your notes and experience. Include thoughts, visions, feelings, and whatever happened to you during your practice. The purpose of this is so that we can reflect on our progress. Look back once we move onto the next week and the next until we are finished with our three weeks.

**Week Two**

Again, you are going to want to create another intent or question, do something different every day. Some ideas may be that you wish to guidance or love through this week. It could also be that you want to implement happiness with everyone you meet or advance in your Reiki healing abilities. Draw the Usui symbol again in front of yourself and move this energy into your heart (Heart Ki). Inhale deeply with your stomach in through your nose and breathe in the essence of this symbol. As you slowly exhale through pursed lips, let the energy overtake your emotions, mental body, and physical body, and then through to your spiritual body. Visualize any unhealthy mental and emotional patterns and then challenge them to transfer them into positive thoughts and emotions. State your intention or question at this moment and sit with the energy for up to 20 minutes (like the first week).

When your mind strays, pull your attention back and focus back to your meditative Reiki session and redraw the Usui symbol three times. Then re-visualize the energy moving to your heart again. Once this is complete, recognize that you're holding and taking in the full love and healing energy of Reiki energy and allow it to be with you throughout your day. In your journal, take note of your experience that you have completed in the last week.

**Week Three**

Begin the session as you have the last 14 days by creating a question of intent, then drawing your Usui symbol. Instead of focusing the Reiki energy into your solar plexus or your heart, this time, you will be focusing it towards your head (Heavenly Ki) and then transferring it to your entire body. This means following the Reiki energy from the crown of your head through and down to your toes. Draw a deep breath in through your nose, pushing your abdomen out, as before and fully accept this energy. As you breathe out through pursed lips, releasing all air in your gut, allow the energy to take over all body matter and expand out into the universe. At this point, you will set forth your intention or ask your question.

Then, visualize the Reiki symbol as a bridge of light. The bridge is from you. It is reaching out into the universe to all time and all space. Allow this bridge of light to carry your Reiki energy through time, such as the past, present, and future. Allow it take over all levels of your consciousness to other dimensions of your physical being. Once this is complete, intentionally let this energy bring your future peace and happiness to you. Lastly, bring yourself and your energy to the present moment. Embrace this for up to twenty minutes. When the session is complete, recognize that you are holding the spiritual healing power of Reiki energy and let it be with you throughout your day. Again, write notes in your journal and reflect on your past records.

This three-week process will allow you to really interpret and possess Reiki healing energy in all your senses. You may feel enlightened or inspired to implement personal growth within yourself in all aspects of universal life. With this acceptance and the power of Reiki healing, you will really be able to focus this type of energy onto your animals, which you will learn how to do in the following chapters of this book.

## SIX

## Reiki Grounding

GROUNDING IS A RELATIVELY SIMPLE PROCESS WHICH IS usually associated by individuals with holistic healing practices such as Reiki. It is a means in which the person would create an imaginary connection with the Earth. In most of the cases, the link would be between the center of the Earth and the root chakra. It would create the relationship between the two. During the process, it would develop the grounding cord which would relieve the energy of other people, increase their emotional health, cleanse the seven chakras, and boost the life force energy from within. The grounding system is used by most of the Reiki practitioners to shift energies from the Earth into the bodies. They also use the method after a Reiki session to eliminate the energies which had been transferred from a person or for strengthening energy.

Although, it might sound like grounding is simple, since people may realize their personal energy levels, the power of the earth energies, and the effects of grounding for their psychological health. However, it is more profound and complicated than that. There are various sources on grounding techniques that have been created and its effects on people.

## Most Common Grounding Technique

Grounding is commonly used by people who are associated with each of the holistic healing concepts out there, such as Yoga and not just by Reiki masters or practitioners. Everyday people may also ground themselves to promote relaxation and reduce stress. The most common type of ground technique that is used is the one in which it involves meditation to connect to the Earth by imagining that roots come out from the body and go deep into the center of the Earth.

For this grounding technique, the person would create a connection with the Earth by imagining a root connection both the center of the root chakra and the Earth. It then uses this connection to transfer the energies of the Earth into the body and the burying of negative energies deep within the Earth. A person can create a strong connection to go as deep within the Earth as the person wants and to secure a connection.

## Cleansing

Once the connection is deep and secure, the person can pull the energies of the Earth through the imaginary root to their base chakra. It would also use the earth energies for cleansing the chakra within the human body. It would then move the energy to the other chakras one after the other until it has reached the head chakra and passed through it.

It would cleanse the chakras using this technique from all negative energies, and it would fill the body with positive earth energies. Once the energies of the Earth reach the head, the person would then resend all the way to the base chakra. This circulation of earth energy with the body would help re-energize the system and help relieve one from all negative energies.

## SEVEN

Grounding Meditation

GROUNDING MEDITATION CAN BE BENEFICIAL FOR LETTING GO of negative energies and reconnecting with the earth. It is used by Reiki and other health practitioners due to its many advantages. Without proper grounding, there would be an excess of fiery energy that would accumulate in the head, and it would cause pressure, headaches, and even hallucination. If you are looking for the ultimate grounding technique, then the following steps will get you to experience an out of this world experience.

1. Find a quiet spot to practice grounding meditation without getting interrupted. One can sit on a chair and maintain a straight back to stay focused. Avoid slouching. Remove the shoes to let the feet fully contact the ground. Rest the hands on the lap.

2. Close the eyes and start to take deep and slow breaths without any force. Breathe in through your nose and exhale through the mouth. Pay attention to breathing. Notice how the chest would expand with each breath, and how it fills the lungs with air until they feel full. Then, see how the lungs relax and allow you to feel relieved when the tightness of the chest is relieved through the mouth. The lungs would start to

feel more alive with every fresh breath. An inhale and exhale considered as a breathing cycle. Make sure to complete at least five of these cycles.

3. When you feel ready, move the attention to the navel. Instead of filling up the chest, let each of the breath fill up the lower abdomen, just about 1.5 inches below the navel. Look at how it gently rises and relaxes when you breathe naturally and mindfully. The breathing would help ease any knots or tightness around each part of the body.

4. As the breath continues, draw attention towards the legs. Feel the thighs and contact them with the knees, ankles, and calves. Feel the temperature and the hardness under the feet. Are they warm or cold? If there is any tension felt, consciously make an effort to relax them. Allow the force of gravity to attract you to the earth.

5. When you start to feel calm and are ready, extend the awareness all the way deeper into the ground with your feet as if they are a majestic redwood tree that has flexible and robust roots. Even if one is sitting in a multi-story building, they should allow the roots to grow and travel all the way down, penetrating through each of the floors in the building until finally reaching deep into the soil. Now, let the roots grow as deep as possible towards the center of the earth. The earth is a source of cooling energy which is often characterized by the color blue. As the roots extend deep within the ground, let them dip into the vast turquoise ocean. Let the refreshing, soothing energy of the energy cool you down through your roots. Trust the wisdom of the body to absorb the fresh energy.

## EIGHT

## Reiki for Domestic Animals

PET ANIMALS FALL UNDER THIS CATEGORY IF THEY ARE domesticated. Domestic refers to the family in a sense. In this regard, domestic animals are family pets that can be cats, dogs, ferrets, birds, reptiles, bugs, spiders, etc. Whatever the case, all domestic animals known as pets are family-related and hold their own unique healing powers within themselves. They feed on their owner's energy and release or transfer their energy onto you to help you feel better.

Before diving into how to heal your pets through Reiki, you first need to understand how to communicate with them. The ability to listen to your internal, instinctive intuition, as a means to know what your pets want. Most body language that comes from your pets is natural to read, such as when they are hungry, excited, or depressed.

You'll find that some body language signs are not so easy to read. For example, when you just come home from a shopping trip, your cat, dog, bird, or any other pet you have, may run up to you and either brush up against you. They may wag their tails excitedly or sit beside you. These are clear signs that they missed you and are happy that you are home.

The subtle signs that we may miss happen because we are

blocked or too busy with our own lives to notice. For example, your pet may be grooming themselves a lot, or pacing more than usual, or even sleeping when they don't usually sleep. Of course, these signs are different for every animal, but you may mistake these signs for something else.

Often, you can tell what your pet's schedule is. You usually know when they sleep, eat, or want attention.

Over time, you really get to know who your animal is and what makes them tick. If any of these habits become unusual for them, then we need to be able to understand and notice them to figure out what the problem is. This is important because most pets and animals, in general, have their own unique way of showing us. Reiki animal healing is about noticing these signs and learning how to solve the problem through love and compassion behind your intent of Reiki.

## Communicating With Your Pet

Everything is made up of energy. If you don't believe me, think about the invisible sensations or vibrations you get when your gut tells you to run. Or upon meeting someone, you might know instantly whether they are easy to talk to or if you want to be closed off to them.

People who struggle with mental illness such as anxiety, borderline personality disorder, PTSD, etc., might experience energy blockages that create mental illness. For example, when you think negatively, you will view the world as negative. When you think positive, the world and the Universe will reward you.

Maybe you and your friend were talking about taking a road trip, and then later by yourself, you thought perhaps it's not the right time right now. Imagine something terrible comes up on the news, such as an unfortunate accident that happened in the place you were planning to go. This is the internal energy that tells you what's going on or what's happening.

Everything we do, think about, and feel is all based around our energy, which is a different perspective, is the law of attraction. Think and do good, the universe will give and show you goodness back.

This is how all animals communicate with the universe. They don't speak our language, but they do understand. Look at a snake, for example. Snakes are mostly blind, but they sense fear through the ground and through the vibrations or pheromones you give off. Why is it that some people can hold a poisonous snake and not be affected or attacked by them? Yet someone who fears them or is at all cautious of the snake, it will go after or try to strike?

Look at dogs or cats, for instance, when you are sad, they feel and feed off that energy. Or when you become angry and frustrated, they also feed off that vibe. They try to make you feel better when you are upset and stay away from you if you are the type of person who likes to be alone when you are angry.

Have you ever been in a sour mood and you were sitting by yourself thinking, I wish I had someone to love me right now, I feel so lonely? Then almost immediately, your pet comes to comfort you. You could almost call this telepathy from an animal to you. Domesticated pets are animals and like people who learn about each other's lives, habits, frustrations, etc. It's about living in the same space and getting to know each other's ways of life as a way to communicate and bond. You may see a lazy dog, then realize they live with a lazy person. Or you may hear a vocal bird if their owner likes to talk to them regularly. Every animal-human relationship is different and unique in its own way. So, is it possible to be able to understand and communicate with your pets? Absolutely.

The question isn't about IF we can communicate, it's HOW we can communicate with our animals. We need to tap into our personal energy, grow our Reiki energy (be connected to the universe), then connect heart to heart, mind to mind, and be one with our pets. As everything is revolved around energy, it's up to you to choose whether to open your mind to that world. Once you do, you can send and receive subliminal or invisible messages efficiently.

Most people have closed their minds because they may have had a bad experience. They were given the wrong mentor, or they were blocked intuitively which shut down all belief that energetic wavelengths even existed. From this, they have now turned skeptical as to whether or not active telepathic communication works. If you are one of these suspicious people, understand this one thing right now: let go of everything you think is correct.

Having these beliefs that you will develop unique gifts or have superpowers or that you will hear the voice of your animals only sets expectations. When it doesn't happen, you become disappointed and will fail. It's like when you look for a lover, they never come, but when you stop looking, the love of your life enters. Or when you're looking for something and can't find it, but when aren't looking for something, it shows up. Whether this is trying too hard, or Murphy's Law, or coincidence--it happens. Animal communication works after you have let go of all your expectations about the process.

One thing is for sure and has been proven correct throughout time. You can never master the art of something unless you don't give up. You must dedicate yourself through knowledge, commitment, practice, and experience. Only then will you learn and grow.

With that said, pet and animal communication takes work and practice. You must tap into your spiritual energy first and be open to new experiences. Be open to the impossible. Learn from your mistakes and try again. If one mentor doesn't work for you, move on. If one blog post, book, or knowledgeable resource doesn't speak to you, go somewhere else. The practice is everything but always keep the focus of your goal and your intent. Once this is in place, you will have the clarity and peace of mind to continue your route towards understanding your pets. You can give back to them through the art of Reiki healing. The art of understanding your pet is by developing your telepathic abilities.

First, the definition of telepathy is mostly being able to see, envision, and feel mental communication without verbal signals. Tele, meaning telephone or wireless vibration through a cellular device or another form of communicating, and pathy, referring to empathy. Empathy is the ability to feel and understand someone else's emotions and experiences through their eyes or energies. Foundationally, this is a form of Reiki healing.

- When close to someone, have you ever called them up randomly and it turned out they were having a tough time?
- How is it that a mother or parent can tell when their child is in trouble or getting into trouble?
- Can you look at a random stranger and just know that they are struggling?

This is telepathy in its first level, as it is first recognizing that we can tap into our intuition or sixth sense. Animals do this instinctively. They are always trying to communicate with you to tell you what's wrong, what makes them happy, what they have been through, what they are feeling, etc.

Animals see and know things that we don't, mainly, they operate on a totally different field, called an energy barrier. Many people mistake their pet's intuition or communication as a coincidence, or they pop up and disappear accidentally. This is not true because as they operate on an energy-based field, they are always paying attention. Simply put, they cannot speak our language and tell us what's going on. But they are observant in everything that happens around them, mostly focusing on you.

To start actually communicating and understanding your pet, talk to them. Don't worry; it's not you being crazy. Verbally talking to your pet before going to the vet or trying something new will allow them to feel more relaxed so they can get the proper treatment. Now you may be thinking, but animals cannot understand our verbal language. It's all about the intent or the message we send through our energy. Although animals cannot know what we are saying, they are instinctively in tune with our body language and our emotions or feelings.

So, if you notice your pet 'out of sorts' speak to them about going to the vet. When we talk to anyone whether that is our mothers, friends, strangers, coworkers, we speak with the intent behind our words. This is why sometimes you come out of a conversation feeling exhilarated or disappointed. It's much more than just emotional intelligence when trying to communicate.

It's the thought of I am passionate or upset about xxx and when you communicate verbally to someone or your pet. Your original feeling behind the words you use will come out in your energy as an invisible layer of excitement form the intent. The goal of passion. Or it will come out as tense and aggressive from the original thought point of being upset.

Therefore, this is why most self-help programs ask you to take some time to think before resolving conflict and always go into an adverse situation with a relaxed state of mind.

Going back to verbally having a discussion with your pet now. Speak to your pet. Whether you are letting them know that you are practicing Reiki healing, tell them. About to take them to the vet? Tell them. Going for a car ride? You got it, tell them. Whatever you are doing that has to do with them, speak to them about it.

The intent behind your verbal language is what they will

feel so that they can go into what will happen next with ease, as you have already had a discussion with them. As this is the first step in communicating with your pets, the more you bond with them in this way, the more you will be able to hear what their needs are. Over time through the transfer of your energy.

By verbally communicating with them, you are enforcing the energy bond between you two. You can tap into your intuitive sixth sense, revolving their needs, wants, and desires. When an animal or pet feels comfortable with you, they will allow you to hear them. That's basically it.

## NINE

## How to Use Reiki for Your Pet

YOU CANNOT HEAL YOUR ANIMAL THROUGH REIKI WITHOUT first knowing how to communicate with your animal. The good news is that regardless of what you learn first—Reiki healing, or animal communication—they go hand in hand. You will know both through learning and experiencing the other. One of the good things about Reiki is that you can heal your animals at any time and practice with them even when they are not ill. You may get the best results when they are sick or have been through something traumatic. The ability to understand and really listen to them will help in your progress towards mastering Reiki healing. So, how do you read an animal to identify their issue? Here are some clear signs, though not a full list:

- If an animal screeches, hisses, growls or runs from you, they are letting you know they do NOT want to be touched. In this case, distant Reiki will be most beneficial.
- If your hands are too close to them during a Reiki session, they may turn and look at you or shift their

position. This is their way of letting you know you are too close for comfort. Lift your hands a few inches away from them and restart.

- When practicing Reiki meditation, or performing a healing session on yourself or someone else, your pet may come to you and brush against you. This is a sign that they want a Reiki session.
- When you develop a close bond with your pet or another animal, they may move or shift for you, as a way to tell you this spot is where I need my healing.

If you groom your pet regularly and are always affectionate with them, they will be the most receptive to Reiki touch healing. However, you can use different Reiki healing techniques that are suitable for each pet. Reiki has three forms: touch, almost touch, a distance above or away from the animal, and distance outside the pet's home. Based on the communication level with your animals in general, you will know what suits their needs best. When introducing Reiki to your pet or someone else's pet you don't know, it's best to go into it cautiously.

You will want their consent before you can do anything. So when you approach a domestic, make sure to move towards them slowly. Talk to the animal in a calming tone, and gradually transfer or develop your energy as a way to let them know what you are going to do. This gives the animal enough time to see if they are comfortable with the idea or not. If you want to skip this process (which is not recommended), you can always beam Reiki to the animal while in the same room.

As stated previously in this book, Reiki is about the intent. It's about grabbing hold of your energy and transferring it to the ill. Throughout the Reiki session, you must channel your highest level of healing energy to your subject. To do this, you ask guidance and give thanks to the universe for allowing you to transfer the positive healing energy to the animal. State your intention loud and clear; why are you treating this pet? What is your role as the Reiki healer? Remember, Reiki healing is not from you but **through** you.

Here are some techniques of Reiki healing:

**Distant Reiki**

Distant Reiki can be done from outside the home and from anywhere in the world. This technique is used for trauma treatment, skeptics, skittish animals, and people with busy working schedules.

**Beaming Reiki**

This technique is used for introducing a nervous or afraid animal in the home to Reiki energy. You would start first by beaming (focusing your Reiki energy) onto the pet. Then while you get closer and closer, give the pet the respect and guidance to be able to trust you to connect and eventually build onto hovering Reiki.

**Hovered Hands Reiki**

This is the transfer of Reiki energy through your etheric energy. You hold your hands a few inches above your pet to help them feel comfortable with the session. Typically, your pet will remain for a more extended period when you practice the hovering technique.

**Reiki Touch**

Just as you would position your hands in the hovering method, you would do this except with hands-on. You are directly connected to them, their minds, their physical body, and their soul. Through Reiki touch, your pet can really feel all of the healing effects from the transfer in energy.

**Group Reiki**

The idea behind group Reiki is for larger animals or animals that feel more comfortable with being around other animals. It's a technique where you send love, compassion, and your intent to a group all at once.

Reiki healing is not to change the dynamics of your pet's

sickness or to slow the process of an upcoming passing. It's to help aid your pet through their experiences in the past or future. Reiki healing may be able to cure your pet's illness. But remember, it is mainly to enhance their lives through love and compassion of their healer.

## Reiki for Cats

As necessary, it is to learn about the Chakras in our own bodies (energy points through our 'vessel'). It is also essential to understand that every animal also has its own Chakras. Cat's, unlike humans, have eight Chakras. The foundation of Reiki is the sole fact that energy is all around us and found in our universal life force.

Just like our Chakras can become blocked, so can the Chakra of a cat or any other animal for that matter. During a Reiki session, the first thing to tune into is your cat's Chakra or energy blockages. You can then unblock these to identify what else could be wrong with them. After the Chakra becomes unblocked, any trauma, tension, injury, illness, or distressing emotions, your cat feels should be lifted.

When practicing Reiki on your cat, get them to lie down comfortably for you. Most of the time, cats are independent and will do their own thing. Through the means of human-animal communication, your cat should know what you are about to do and will cooperate as they are very susceptible to receiving energy. Your Reiki session should take no longer than an hour, but most times it could last only ten to fifteen minutes. The really great thing about Reiki healing practice is that you don't have to guess when your pet is finished. They will get up and walk away when they have received enough energy from you. So, how do you start performing Reiki on your cat?

Earlier, you learned the different Reiki meditations to develop and hold the universal energy of Reiki within yourself. Drawing back to this chapter, re-read the Center Finger Method and figure out what you have blocked within yourself first.

Through the **21-Day Reiki Meditation** practice, you will have learned how to identify where your blockages were. Through those weeks, you would have been able to unblock yourself. Now you can focus on the healing of others, such as with your pets and animals. After unblocking yourself and taking in the Reiki energy, it is time to bring your cat into the equation.

- Place your hands on or above your cat. Breathe in and follow the Reiki light to your hands and refocus the light just above your pet.
- Let the energy attach or flow into and through your cat naturally. Take a deep breath and concentrate this energy force into your cat (or animal) and try to interpret what your cat is telling you.
- Once you feel the Reiki energy is being transferred at a constant flow from yourself to your feline, state your intent.
- The intent could be identifying where your cat's blockages are, what type of illness or injury it feels, or just healing in general. Let the cat 'telepathically' communicate with you through this experience.
- End the session by letting go of your energy into your cat and visualizing the light leaving your hands and into your feline friend. Take a deep breath, and then thank the universe for the ability to heal and transfer your energy to your pet. Or otherwise follow the last step in Chapter Two, Sealing Off Energy.

The energy of Reiki is non-invasive and only allows us to gain knowledge of what our subject wants us to know. Your cat can decide to bring images to your mind concerning their past experiences, or about what they need in this particular session on its own. Don't worry if your cat walks away if you are not done. Sometimes we can misjudge how much healing they need, so what works for them is what only they know, and they will walk away if they feel they have had enough. Through this process, you must trust that your energy is going to the spots on your pet that it needs to go. When the healing is complete, the energy flow will cut itself off, therefore leaving you with gratitude that it worked.

## The Chakras of Your Cat

There are eight Chakras in your feline friend. Chakra means 'Wheels of Light or Life' because it is crucial to the healthy life cycle of all that exists—including your cat. Chakras receive, absorb, and hold life force energy (Reiki). While humans have to practice, develop, and become in tune with their Chakras, cats and animals are already instinctually inclined to it. They feed off of and act upon what their energy points, Chakra points, are doing. If one chakra is blocked, your cat may show it in the signs of illness, or depression. Here are the eight Chakra points in your cat.

**First Chakra, Root**: A blockage in this Chakra and your cat may show greed, fear, lethargy, or become over or underweight. This is the base of your cat's energy and where they express balance or imbalance the most. It is located at the bottom of your cat's spine, just before the tail.

**Second Chakra, Sacral**: Your cat may seem restless, overly vocal, emotional, anxious, or abnormally skittish if this Chakra is imbalanced or blocked. The sacral, also known as sexual progression, allows your cat to breed and become or develop confidence. The Sacral is located in the lower abdomen close to the reproductive system.

**Third Chakra, Solar Plexus**: A solar plexus blockage may consist of signs of aggression, moodiness, laziness, or depression. It is located just below the shoulder blades and can represent digestive problems, diabetes, lack of confidence, or obsessive behavior.

**Fourth Chakra, Heart**: The location of this Chakra lies in the chest and heart area. An imbalance can manifest itself with signs of depression, nervous energy, blood disorders, distress, and the inability to bond with others.

**Fifth Chakra, Throat**: Located in the neck and throat area. Signs of a blocked fifth Chakra can come as a lack of or excessive vocalization, lack of communication, withdrawn attitude, teething, and behavioral problems.

**Sixth Chakra, Third Eye**: Located in between the brows, the sixth Chakra, being the third eye imbalance consists of eye problems, headaches, inability or struggle with focusing, loss of hair, and PTSD pain.

**Seventh Chakra, Crown**: An imbalance of the seventh Chakra can be visible when your cat is feeling confused, anxious. They may be having sudden panic attacks, separation issues, stress shown through aggression, and restlessness. The crown is located at the top of the head in between the ears.

**Eighth Chakra, Brachial**: Your cat will show signs of a blocked brachial by withdrawing from you, distance in affection, and moodiness. The eighth Chakra is located at the very tip of their snout.

Learning the different locations of your felines Chakras will help you in your Reiki healing practice. As you move your hands along them, you will be able to sense the blockage through the transfer in energy. It also helps to be able to understand your cat's personality and behaviors so that when you notice any of the imbalanced signs. You will be able to tap into that and give them Reiki healing on your own time.

## Reiki for Dogs

What you have learned thus far essentially is how it goes for all pets. You first need to learn how to communicate with them. Then you need to hold Reiki healing within yourself to be able to transfer it to your pet. Your dog, along with other small animals, all have Chakras. However, while some animals have eight Chakras, your dog only has seven, like you, while some other animals actually have nine Chakras.

For all pets and animals, Reiki has many benefits, it can:
Ease pain

- Correct behavioral problems
- Boost immunity
- Decrease healing time for any injury or medication intake
- Remove Chakra or energy blockages
- Promote physical and mental well-being
- Reduce distress and emotional baggage
- Strengthen the bond between animal and human interaction

For humans, a Reiki session involves the patient lying down while the practitioner moves their hands across the Chakra points of the patient's body. The intent is to draw out the negative or blocked energy then sweep it into the universe to get rid of it and end the session. For a dog, they may prefer to have Reiki used on them from a distance through Reiki beaming or from a different location entirely.

The session will start as the practitioner (you), invite the canine to come into the same room, and sit beside them. Just like a cat, the dog will then reassure using body language as to when to begin and will take as much energy as they feel fit or are comfortable with. Only if a dog wants to be touched can you actually come in contact them and use the hands-on experience with your animal. Generally speaking, there are two main Reiki techniques used on dogs: relaxation and emotional release.

Whether or not you are a master in Reiki, your dog can still benefit from the touch of your hands. Provided that internal intent is clear as to what you want to achieve for your dog through the experience.

### Relaxation

Start at the neck and head area of your canine companion and slowly move your hand down your dog's back, ending the touch at the base of their tail. Stop at each Chakra point in their body (same as a cat's) and imagine your Reiki energy going into these points. Take in a deep breath, and then as you exhale, imagine your own energy and relaxed vibes going into your pooch. The focal points you should be stopping and releasing your energy on are the shoulders, midsection, and lower back area. For each region, you will hold your hands on either side of their body. Exhale your energy into their body.

### Emotional Healing

Emotional healing is based on the way you place your hands on your pup. In the same way as before, you will have to get them relaxed or lying down so that they are comfortable. Find your own energy within yourself and take a deep breath before you start. As you place your hands on your puppy's head, breathe your energy following the light into your dog. For emotional healing, you are going to put one hand on your dog's back between the shoulders and one hand on their chest. Or, you can choose to place one hand on the top of your dog's head between their ears and one on their chest. Keep your hands placed there and imagine the inner light of Reiki energy going into your dog. Ask or state your intent at this point and continue moving your hands down your dog.

To end the Reiki healing session, if they haven't walked away, take a deep breath. Once you reach the base of your dog's tail, exhale the remainder of your energy imagining it flows directly into your dog. Shake the excess negative energy off and out into the universe, and then give thanks and compassion to your surroundings, yourself, and your pooch.

The intent behind every Reiki healing session will solely depend on your own personal positivity. There are no clear signs as to if Reiki works, but it doesn't mean that nothing happened. Every time you practice this with your pet or animal, your bond will get stronger. At that point, you will be able to tune into their specific needs easily.

## Reiki in General

When considering Reiki on small animals, including birds, rodents, reptiles, bugs, etc. generally speaking, it is used in the same five techniques mentioned with similar benefits. Smaller animals have smaller bodies and different dynamics to their system. When dealing with smaller animals, you can choose to hold them in your one hand. Hover over their backs with your other, or you can choose to Reiki heal from a distance if they have cages or a place inside your home. As long as you are following your intent and implementing it into your Reiki routine, it is almost fully guaranteed to work. The best things you can do for your animals are to practice your own self-care. Develop your personal spirituality so that your Reiki session will be powerful.

Reiki healing for domestic animals is not the same as for other animals like horses or pets that belong outside. Sick or senior pets may benefit more from a distance Reiki or hovering Reiki as some joints may be too sensitive for you to touch.

Bigger animals, such as horses need attention in other

areas. The practice may take longer than those that live with you inside your house because of their size. No matter what, the practice of Reiki works in its own way, and all you need to do is obtain it and release it. The rest of the routine will happen naturally.

# TEN

## Reiki for Sick Animals

As mentioned previously, Reiki healing is beneficial to all life forces on Earth. These life forces consist of plants, animals, humans, and any other living thing created on the planet. The reason Reiki is so beneficial is that it can be done on almost any animal. Ranging from farm animals such as horses and sheep or chickens to smaller animals such as mice, ferrets, and guinea pigs.

Every animal in between like dogs, cats, tigers, reptiles, and monkeys can also benefit because it can be done from far away or up close and personal. Almost every animal on this planet operates on an energy wavelength that is sometimes difficult for people to wrap their minds around.

Reiki will never harm your animal. In fact, it is the most natural aid in healing diseases like cancer and arthritis to solving mental issues such as behavioral problems and depression. It's the act in which you transfer energy from yourself drawing from the universe into your subject and through that process, Reiki will do most of the work. Reiki finds the problem, takes your energy and the energy surrounding you, and gives strength and wellness to the animal you are working on. The animal senses these invisible vibrations and can also choose for themselves how much for how long they want to take from you.

All you or the practitioner does is awake the intuition. Open the mind to the belief in this energy force. Hold the intention of compassion and healing behind the practice. Since Reiki is closely related to the energy points inside every being the Chakras, it finds the blockage and stimulates the area to work again or become unblocked. If your pet or an animal you know or don't know is sick, injured, or a senior, Reiki is there to ease the transition toward what happens next. Essentially, Reiki brings peace, comfort, relaxation, emotional and mental healing, and reduced physical pain.

## ELEVEN

## Reiki for Senior Animals

Senior animals struggle with walking around. They don't possess the energy they once did, and it can really do a number on their emotional and mental health. That puppy that you first brought home is no longer bouncing with excitement, or that kitten that you adopted thirteen years ago is no longer playful. You reminisce on so many memories and good times together but feel pain in your heart as you watch them become slower every day. They are on medication to help with their joints, and maybe you have had to buy stairs so they can lay with you on your furniture.

The time is here; your pet is a senior. In this stage of their lives, it is essential to support them through the difficult time they are experiencing. Your mouse or ferret may not be able to speak verbally to you. Despite that, within everything you have learned thus far from Reiki, you already know what they are thinking and feeling. Reiki therapy is so helpful for these aging horses and elderly sheep. Whatever pet you have, it is now the best time to welcome Reiki into your lives. Here is why:

**Pain Relief**

When we are children, we experience growing pains or restless leg syndrome. When we become teenagers, we may suffer from headaches or back pain. As we age into adults, we can experience neck-aches, joint problems, arthritis, etc. Finally, as an elder, it is more than likely we need to take pills like Tylenol or muscle relaxers to escape our body pain. Something which radiates through us all the time. Our animals go through these same stages of emotions throughout their lives. The most significant difference is that they cannot tell us what is wrong unless we tap into the communication between human and animal. Reiki helps injuries from aching bones heal faster. Just as cortisol hormones rise in us when we feel stressed, it does the same for our senior animals. Animals can become stressed when they cannot perform for us like they once did. Reiki has proven to change these stress-induced hormones for an amount of time to relax and bring peace of mind to our senior pets.

To really help our senior animals, we need to Reiki transfer healing energy to them daily. Again, whatever treatments the vet has prescribed should never be replaced by Reiki. Reiki aids in helping them feel comfortable. Senior animals like to sleep and rest, but with their continuous pain, they may find it very difficult to do so. With Reiki, they can feel more relaxed because their joint pains are not as bad as if you didn't Reiki heal.

### Emotional Well-Being

The older we become, the more at risk we become for Alzheimer's and dementia. We may become very forgetful or even confused. Our emotions become higher, and our bodies become slower. So, if this happens to us, can you imagine what your senior animal is going through? Have you noticed your dog bump into things due to blindness? Maybe you have seen your cat walk into the kitchen but stand there dazed because of forgetfulness. Reiki helps with emotional well-being by giving your pet a sense of deep peace and relaxation, which actually promotes focus and concentration. To know whether or not Reiki is working, there are a few clear signs.

These signs might include your pet lying down in front of you to gain your healing energy. Or, they may breathe out a sigh of relief while in the session.

**Fear Reduction**

Fear comes with age due to the aging brain. Things you may not have feared before may become a really intense emotion for you now. For example, when you are an adolescent, you may enjoy going to an amusement park and being in a large group of crowds for the excitement and thrill of everything you are experiencing.

Now, as a retired senior, going to an amusement park or being in groups of people is scary due to the stress that comes with it. This is the same for our pets. They may fear car rides but loved them before. They may fear meeting other animals, whereas they had the patience for it earlier. They may jump at loud noises, whereas before it never seemed to bother them.

Being fearful of these things can lead to heightened levels of anxiety, which causes stress and mental blockages. Reiki helps reverse these types of blockages and leaves your senior pet feeling relaxed. Just in case they do need to meet another animal or go for a car ride to the vet.

Aggression in older animals is the number one response to acting out of fear. Behavioral problems may arise as well with the animal peeing inside, not wanting to go outside, excessive vocalization, pacing, sleep disturbances, or trouble eating. It's not a fun experience for them. Reiki helps with reducing the fear that is felt from old age by putting your pet in a meditative state. This way, they can happily feel less pain as they drift off to sleep, waiting to pass away. It may also increase their appetite since they feel better after a Reiki session.

**Dying**

Almost all humans fear the unknown. We fear what we cannot control and part of that fear, as we become elderly, is death. Is it time for your feline friend or canine companion, or rodent playmate to pass on? You may know it's time for them to go, but they may be holding on a little longer for your sake. Death brings upon sadness and grief. However, death also brings new beginnings and learning experiences. Reiki helps your animal feel better about passing away, mainly when you perform the Reiki. Instead of passing on in pain, emotional baggage, and spiritual blockage, Reiki can help them feel at peace with the idea of moving on. Reiki offers grounding and serenity to their mind and body so that it is easier for them to let go. Not only has Reiki proven to be helpful in the passing away process for your animals, but it has also shown to give you some closure as well. Yes, you may feel sad and upset that your best friend is gone. But with using Reiki healing for yourself and through the process, you can come to terms with it leaving you with a sense of enlightenment.

When you look at the positives, animals generally never complain. They love what they have. Your pets appreciate you, and they have a tendency to just live in the moment. As they age, things become more confusing, and life generally becomes more complicated than it used to be. With Reiki, it helps them to accept what is happening right now and gives them the strength to cope with their progressive changes.

# TWELVE

## Reiki for Injured Animals

WHEN IT COMES TO SPIRITUAL HEALING OR ANY TYPE OF healing, Reiki can be looked at as a form of acupuncture, acupressure, and chiropractic services. Reiki was developed out of what's called 'Qigong,' a parent of Tai Chi, and has become a wellness technique for both animal and human health and growth. This system uses the body's energetic system revolving around the Chakras.

This revolving area is also called the meridian system. Instead of using needles or hot rocks on the body, Reiki stimulates the flow of energy (Ki) in the body through different hand gestures using the flow of one's own energy to transfer into their subject. From this transfer of energy, the subject's body takes the healing energy and places it wherever there are imbalances or blockages in the energetic Chakras.

Anyone who experiences Reiki has said or shown that it is incredibly relaxing, bringing the patient (animal and human) to another level of meditation through the guidance and support of the practitioner. The patients benefit from Reiki because it doesn't matter whether they are ill, weak, sore, mentally ill, or emotionally unwell. Reiki is a non-harmful exercise in developing growth wellness in an individual.

Through the gentle gestures of the Reiki practice, the body is guided to recover whatever energy imbalance it may be suffering with. When an animal is injured or recuperating after surgery, Reiki can balance blood pressure, strengthen the immune response for faster healing, and rejuvenating sleep.

It helps the animal absorb their vitamins through food while increasing their appetite if it was lost. It also helps them feel more comfortable before, during, and after a procedure like surgery or chemotherapy for cancer. Studies show that Reiki helps with child labor in both animals and humans, making for speedy recovery afterward and less pain during the childbirth.

If we take Reiki out of the equation and just rely on facts around science and research, people who are calmer and more relaxed can get through conflict in relationships, develop a more profound sense of inner peace, and make it through past trauma easier. People or animals regularly go to vets and doctors to get prescription medication to help aid or heal in forms of muscle relaxers, depressive medicines, vitamins, etc.

Reiki skips these steps (but is not replaced by them) and balances the mind so that the body can enjoy the intake of the healing. Then it can progress and do what it needs to do to heal. Anyone can learn Reiki by developing an open mind and learning their inner spirituality. It can lead people to new beginnings and other spiritual paths in their lives.

Animals are just as equal to humans in the sense that they experience and go through changes and challenges as we do. Through the practice of Reiki, which essentially is a relaxation aid, it opens the minds of your subjects to cure and help with the internal growth of injury or other imbalances through the energetic system.

When anxiety and stress are reduced through the guide of Reiki healing the body can develop more energy to tackle whatever diseases or injuries it is facing. Reiki activates the automatic response of different parts of the body so that the body can do its job in healing itself. This happens through balancing the imbalances in our Chakras. Because Reiki is a safe, non-invasive practice, it is so quickly developed and learned by anyone open to the idea of it. With that being said, Reiki helps in all aspects of your life. It can improve the lives of your patients or pets too.

## THIRTEEN

# Reiki for Dying Pets

THE ABILITY TO CONNECT WITH OUR ANIMALS CAN EITHER HELP our pet pass on or challenge our pet to pass away. This is because when we are so close to our animals. They can sense our frustrations, our sadness, our anger, and our pain from knowing that they are getting ready to die. Although this is a painful and upsetting process for both owner and pet, it's the way of life, and it represents new beginnings and prosperity. Reiki helps relax our feelings around the process, which then gives our animals a more relaxed time accepting the process of what is to come. If you are the Reiki practitioner for your animal in this passing away process, there are a few things you should know first.

## Let Go of Your Anger

Sometimes we are angry with ourselves due to the selfishness of not seeing our pets suffering earlier. We may want to keep them around a little longer, or we may have ignored their signs because of our own denial. Before practicing Reiki on your animal, it is essential to let go of all anger, as you do not want your pet to feed off this energy. Develop a mindset to be comfortable with what has happened, what is happening, and what will happen. When you spend an unnecessary quantity of time focusing on your anger, it takes away the support you could be giving to your animal in this challenging time.

## Let Go of Your Worry Today

It is essential to boost your own emotions and look at this experience as positive as you possibly can to help ease your pet's transition. Part of this process is to let go of your fear and worries revolving around the process. Remember to be completely present with your animal and for the moment, let go of all concerns within yourself. Do not question the process; do not think about what happens next. Feed your positive vibes into your pet and help them relax into their transition.

## Develop Humbleness

Being humble is about letting go of all control. You may wish or pray for the ability to make things easier for your pet and yourself. Despite that, animals will transition into dying on their own terms as quickly or complicated as they prefer. They will absorb your energy as needed and go on their own terms. When we learn to be grateful in this moment for them, we develop our own sense of awareness that comes with enlightenment after the fact.

## Be Honest

All relationships and bonds come from a more profound trust level. When you can be honest and trust yourself through this process, your pet will feel the same. Do not avoid, push away, or ignore any feelings you have; instead, embrace them and let them out. This is how you can show utmost honesty towards yourself and your pet. Once your pet has fully transitioned, let go of all your emotions. Feel the joy, feel sadness, feel the energy, feel compassion, and feel whatever it is that you are going to feel. It is the first step in letting go. Remember the experiences you have had, cherish the memories, and be thankful for the help and support your animal needed.

## Implement Compassion

What you know now is that you cannot fix or change the circumstances. Whether your animal is old, sick, mentally ill, handicapped, or anything in between, you personally couldn't have changed a thing. Be one with this thought and mindset, and in this way, you will develop compassion and forgiveness for yourself. Develop the state of mind that you love your animal and they love you equally, and when it's time, only they will know. So prepare yourself for the compassion that you can give to yourself. By giving compassion and feeling empathetic, your animal will have an easier time transitioning into their dying process. Once they have passed away, let go of all your regret and guilt.

Every animal, whether that is a horse, dog, mouse, snake, or anything in between, holds the power of having automatic energy forces that they communicate with us through a different field. They know when we are emotionally exhausted and when we are in physical pain. They know when we are mentally unwell, and if we let them, they hold power to heal us. If they allow us, we can tap into this energy field that they regulate. They will permit us to help them in whatever they are trying to overcome.

We can help animals with all of their challenges. Such as attending to their suffering when they are injured. Your pet's emotions when they are stressed. Their pain when they are weak. We can do this through Reiki. If you think about it, Reiki is our way of giving back to our animals. They are always healing us in ways we can't imagine or even see. When we experience our own energy healing, we can implement Reiki into our animals as a way of healing to the highest form. Which primarily will aid them throughout their life's challenges.

## FOURTEEN

## Dealing with Grief for the Loss of a Pet

PETS ARE SURELY A BUNDLE OF JOY. THEY ARE ALWAYS delighted to see you whenever you return home from work or school. Their excitement is so evident that you can't help but feel the love. However, losing a pet can be one of the hardest experiences for an individual. After all, a pet is just like a child. The way through which people grieve differs from person to person, and some people find the loss of a pet comes in different stages where they experience feelings of denial, guilt, anger, depression and finally acceptance.

On the other hand, some people might discover that their grief has a cynical effect on them. There are highs and lows. The lows would usually be more profound and more prolonged in the starting, but would later become shorter and less intense. However, even as the years pass by, a special anniversary or date can quickly spark up memories which trigger a strong sense of sadness.

### Coping With the Grief

Grief and sorrow are natural and healthy responses to death. Grief for animal companies can take some time to deal with.

However, there are specific healthy ways to cope with loss and grief. The following suggestions are proven to be helpful.

## Don't Allow Anyone to Tell You How to Feel

Your grief is yours, and no one can tell you when it is time for you to move on. They cannot ask you to get over it. We all deal with grief in our own way, which is why it is essential to let yourself feel whatever you feel to cope with the loss. There is no need to feel any type of embarrassment. It is perfectly fine to feel angry or wanting to cry and not wanting to cry. It is also fine to find moments of joy.

## Connect With Others That Have Lost Pets Too

There are many online forums for pets and pet loss hotlines. Pet loss support groups are also there to allow you to cope with people that are going through similar pain. There is a respite in plurality. Sometimes, friends and family members might not be as sympathetic to pet loss, which is why finding someone who is, is vital. When a person has suffered a similar experience, they would better understand your pain and help you deal with the grief.

## Rituals Help Healing

Funerals help you and the family members to express the feeling of grief openly. Ignore the people that think it is inappropriate to hold a funeral for your pet and do whatever makes you feel better.

## Look After Yourself

Ultimately, when it comes to grief over the loss of a pet, at the end of the day, the stress may often deplete your emotional reserves and energy. This is why it is essential to look after your emotional and physical needs. Spend some time with the people that care and love you. Get some sleep and eat a healthy diet.

## FIFTEEN

## Coping with Compassion Fatigue

As much as you may want to help an animal, you must also take care of yourself. A common side effect of caring for someone that is in need is compassion fatigue. It does lead to emotional and physical exhaustion while reducing the ability to empathize. It is highly prevalent among nurses, doctors, and related caretaker practitioners. Another name for the condition is secondary traumatic stress. In simple words, one can get stressed by continuously wanting to help or helping others that are suffering. If you are suffering from compassion fatigue, then this post is just what you need to be reading. The best ways to cope with compassion fatigue are discussed as follows.

### Be Aware of the Changes in Your Level of Compassion Fatigue

The thing about looking after and caring for animals is that how one feels towards it and their level of stress changes from day to day depending on the health of the patient. This is why it is crucial to make notes about how you feel regularly and track the stress as well as compassion fatigue levels.

The simplest way to do this is by rating how you feel from 1-10. It is possible for you to feel overwhelmed or irritated, as well as have trouble sleeping due to the constant worry. By keeping an eye on the compassion fatigue levels, it allows you to notice and take action before reaching a severe stage such as a 9 or a 10.

## Make Self-Care A Priority

Taking care of oneself should be a priority. Self-care is vital for long term caregiving. It helps keep you physically and mentally healthy and also protects you against compassion fatigue.

One may feel selfish to take time for them, but if they feel run-down or overwhelmed and easily irritable, then that would most definitely come through when caring for the older adult. Besides, when one feels healthy, they can provide better care. Although every person has a different of taking care of themselves, the following are the best way to do so.

- Find ways through which to take breaks from caregiving such as respite care.
- Get help with household or caregiving tasks.
- Take time for yourself every day, even if it is just a few minutes.
- Have a good sleep routine in place and try to aim for high-quality sleep as much as possible.
- Eat a healthy diet.
- Exercise regularly.

## Spend Time with Friends

Perhaps, the best way to cope with compassion fatigue is by maintaining a balance between caregiving and your social connections. When you spend time with friends, it helps prevent depression, isolation, and loneliness.

Chat with friends, share a meal, or just take a walk together, all these help you de-stress and allow you to take a break from caregiving worries.

## Spend Time on Hobbies

Being there for a sick pet or animal does not suggest that you should give up on the things that you enjoy. In fact, it is essential for you to regularly take time to pursue your hobbies and activities that allow you to relax and replenish.

## SIXTEEN

## Reiki Case Studies

FOR THE SKEPTICS OUT THERE WHO STILL DON'T BELIEVE THE magic of Reiki, case studies are illustrating that Reiki healing energy can work. What I find so amazing about Reiki is that not a lot of training is needed for Reiki. As long as you understand how to tap into your own energy, you can just transfer it to your animals, and Reiki healing does the rest. It's easy to learn, easy to tap into and take a lot of practice and dedication to master. However, before we dive right into case studies, I would like to discuss how Reiki works on horses, as horses are quite large spiritual animals. This discussion on Reiki in horses will lead to a dialogue about treating horses. Next we will move into case studies of various other animals.

### Reiki for Horses

As with most animals, energy flows through their bodies like an invisible current. And like most animals, a lot can interfere with the flow of this, such as physical injuries, trauma, nutritional changes, training issues, or even a few of these combined. When an energy point in a horse is blocked, it can cause physical, mental, or behavioral problems just like having these problems can cause a Chakra blockage. Reiki helps keep this in check and balanced so that the horse can do its job better and focus on its training with its owner. Reiki for a horse is also known as Equine Reiki. It restores the energy in the horse that has been blocked or diminished. If a horse has experienced any trauma in its life, the horse will develop some behavioral problems or possibly PTSD and react to sounds, scents, or new experiences. This can quickly aggravate a horse and make it not listen to you. Reiki helps the horse cope with the trauma and releases the emotional attachments holding onto these memories. Thus behavioral problems become manageable rather than destructible. Remember this: a happy horse means a calmer and more relaxed owner. When the owner is composed and patient, the horse will do its job and follow the lead.

All the things that Reiki does for other animals such as dogs, cats, rodents, or bugs, it also does for horses. A horse's Chakras and energy points are located in the same places as a cat's. Equine Reiki can help the owner save money on vet bills because it boosts immunity. As a result, the chances of your horse getting sick before a big show or rodeo is slimmer. Medication for horses can often be in large doses, which can make a horse feel uneasy or nauseous. By using Equine Reiki, the horse can get up and go in a matter of minutes, as the energy intake it gains from you is also a boost in mood and energy.

Laura Borrowdale (2017) wrote an article on her experience with an experienced Equine Reiki trainer. She saw the magic of how Reiki was done on her own horse through a woman named Nia. Once she gained an opportunity to talk about the session, she asked Nia a few questions. I have extracted some beneficial information from their questions and answers to support you, as you understand Reiki on larger animals, such as horses.

Laura was first curious about how Nia, the Equine Reiki

practitioner, experiences the guiding relationship between a horse and the Reiki practitioner. Nia explained that it can go either way, such as Reiki works. Maybe the animal will guide your energy, or you guide it.

They also discussed visualizations and what a Reiki healer might see during a session. Nia experiences visualizations in a few different ways. It might be visualizing exactly where the horse hurts, an emotional release, or a trauma. As you can imagine, these visualizations can be painful for the one practicing Reiki healing.

You might be wondering what a horse looks like when it is being healed with Reiki. Nia notices it in a horse's eyes, as they soften; their heads, as it droops; and their entire body, as they relax.

Laura found Nia through a social feed on Facebook through her mom. Laura had been looking for a practitioner to do Reiki on her horse for quite some time. This just happens to be a common occurrence for people looking for Reiki healers. Nia also says the reason it is so tough to find Reiki healers in the world is that Reiki is not scientifically backed. Also, because as much as you can be a Reiki healer yourself, it's quite tricky to have the qualifications. Then you can make known that you are a Reiki healer for others.

## Mick - Nine-Month-Old Mixed Boxer

Mick, a mixed-breed cross boxer is a rescue animal as he was locked in a kennel by a family in Hungary. The family went on vacation to Paros Island. While Mick was on the trip, he was locked in a kennel with no light or sound for ten hours. Once landed, Mick appeared fearful, aggressive, and anxious to the family. A Reiki practitioner named Trish was called to meet them and hopefully fix or heal the problem; the appointment was made to meet Trish at her house.

Before the appointment, she did a Reiki distance healing

for the problem, explaining that she grounded herself first before starting and then started meditating. She used a stuffed animal as a visualization of the dog to help her reach Mick. Additionally, she used Reiki symbols to be able to connect with Mick since she hadn't met him yet. During the distant Reiki session, she opened her heart and felt an immediate connection to Mick. She felt his anxiety and also found that he was very unsure of his surroundings.

In this case study, Trish announced that animals can receive symbols and images, so that's what she did. Trish sent him animals playing ball with children. A bed with a dog sleeping, as well as other animals who were cuddling close together. As Trish continued her distance Reiki session, she sensed Mick feeling more relaxed and at peace. She then thanked Mick for allowing her to transfer her energy to him and ended the session.

On the day of the appointment with Mick and his family, Trish spent the time before the Reiki session meditating and grounding herself using visualization and intention. Every morning Trish says a prayer and positive affirmations. She communicates only the good that she wants to see. Trish uses words that are only positive when she partakes in her adventures. Her intent behind doing this is so that she can transfer this light and positive energy into her Reiki practice. Before the family arrived at her place, she mixed lavender and distilled water and sprayed the scent wherever she would be sitting. Lavender is a calming scent which makes an animal feel more comfortable and at home during a Reiki session.

When the family arrived at Trish's place, Mick instantly recognized her connection to him and jumped happily all around her. The family was shocked and then went together to her office. Trish asked the family about behavioral problems, medical history, nutrition, as well as how they treat and connect with Mick. After this, Trish explained what Reiki is and that animals are susceptible to this type of energy. When the session finally began, Trish sat in front of Mick on the floor and started with meditation and centering. She grounded herself and sent calming energy to her surroundings. When she sent her own energy to Mick, the boxer sat in front of her.

Throughout the session, Mick would lay down, stretch out, and move around a bit. After the session was over, Trish recommended the family to use the Bach Flower Rescue Remedy as needed with Mick. It's a rescue remedy for animals and people who have heightened anxiety. It restores their place of calm and supports them through any emotional or mental blockage. Trish then gave the family training tips and how to use a clicker with Mick.

Not only was the family relieved to have their dog Mick back to his original happiness, but Mick was also grateful for undergoing such an experience.

## Cleo's Reiki Session

Cleo is a female Rottweiler that was rescued from abuse and aggression in June 2016. For six months since her rescue, Cleo has run around in a rampage full of aggressiveness, barking excessively, and losing a lot of weight. Joanna, a Reiki practitioner, mentioned that when she met Cleo, she sat in front of her cage and mindfully let her know that she was beautiful. After that, Joanna's energy only strengthened and expanded. Joanna sat on the outside of the fence from Cleo, in which she ran, and meditated. Joanna said she was the earth, the air, the grass, and everything in between. The intent Joanna held with her was that Cleo was beautiful, but she continued to meditate without judgment and solely with love.

Joanna visualized love all around Cleo as she ran around and barked. She felt this best to create love and serenity around Cleo rather than directly on Cleo because at first there was absolutely no contact. Eventually, Joanna imagined touching Cleo with this love and peace. She envisioned Cleo engulfed in this light. Cleo then ran up to the fence where Joanna was, barked once, and then ran away again. Over time, Cleo began to calm down. Eventually, the female Rottweiler came to the fence on and off, continuously watching Joanna. Joanna stayed with Cleo for forty minutes. A staff member who was with Cleo every day had attended this experience. She said that Cleo had never acted this way with anyone before. At the end of her first day with Cleo, she began to walk away while looking at Cleo (not directly in her eyes) until she was away from the fence.

There did more than one session, and every session Joanna came back, and Reiki healed, Cleo became more and more relaxed and cured. The second day Cleo and Joanna sat parallel to each other, embracing the love of the Reiki healing just as one unity together. They were both above their thoughts, feelings, and pain; instead, they were only present with one another. Upon many more Reiki sessions, Cleo is now a dog that can trust in people and have gratitude for everything. Cleo is now so open and has no problem being around others without the aggressive or anxious behavior she showed when she first arrived at the shelter.

## Reiki for Mussel and Oyster

Mussel and Oyster are two shelter animal cats that suffer from Cerebellar Hypoplasia. This disorder causes them to wobble and shake as they walk or move. They were young kittens under a year old, and if they were not adopted out before their first year, they would be euthanized. They had been in the Baltimore shelter for five months until Dulcinea, a Reiki healer, came to visit. During Dulcinea's first session with the kittens, Mussel and Oyster were very reserved and did not want to meet or come close at all. Once Dulcinea started her Reiki meditation after fifteen minutes had gone by, she noticed that both kittens were napping. Before she left, she took a minute to thank them and quietly exited their area.

The second time Dulcinea came around, she brought a cushion to sit on for the meditative practice. Immediately after she sat down and placed herself comfortably, Mussel came to sit with her in her lap. Dulcinea's Reiki session caused Mussel to purr noticeably loud, which also allowed Dulcinea to dive deeper into the meditation.

The third time Dulcinea came back for Reiki healing, she had noticed Mussel's head shaking was a lot less noticeable than before. When he walked around to eat or play, he was much more stable in his balance as well. The third session, Oyster was napping, but once she awoke, she came to Dulcinea also. After a couple minutes into the third Reiki session, Dulcinea noticed Oyster grab a drink and eat some food with much less shake and wobble than the first day. As Oyster wandered around the room, Dulcinea let her Reiki energy travel as it needed and witnessed calmness and peace in both the kittens. Dulcinea noticed that for forty-five minutes, both kittens maintained balance and their shaking during walk or play became were less and less as she continued her Reiki healing.

That week both Mussel and Oyster were adopted into a loving and forever home.

## Tug's Arthritis

Aileen is a founder and owner of Hoof, Paw, and Claw in Northborough, Massachusetts. She masters in Reiki as she has practiced since 1996. She is also a teacher in Reiki and animal communication. Here is her success story on Tug, a mini bull terrier and how Reiki helped cure his arthritis.

Aileen was contacted by Tug's owner and requested that she ease her ten-year-old dog's pain from arthritis. The first session was in person, and Tug opened up to the Reiki energy immediately. On Aileen's first-time meeting Tug, she started her practice and Tug laid down in front of her with his hind legs outstretched. Aileen soaked up all the energy everywhere she touched him. Ten minutes later, Tug was fast asleep. The day after the first session, he slept for several hours after and immediately after Tug awoke from his slumber, he was full of life and energy. The effects of Aileen's Reiki healing energy stayed with Tug for a little over a week, which made his feet and arthritis seem almost unnoticeable as he leaped and played.

Aileen treats Tug for his arthritis and pain regularly through distance Reiki and also in person using hands-on Reiki. Tug's owner says that she has noticed that on the distance Reiki days her mini terrier likes to curl up in her lap. As soon as the session ends, he gets up and has a snack.

Through this experience with Tug, the ten-year-old mini terrier has had little to no pain with his arthritis, and he acts as if he is a puppy again. He has more energy to run around, and he doesn't lie around all day whining about his joints. Reiki for Tug has been a miracle for everyone involved.

## SEVENTEEN

# The Five Traditional Usui Reiki Symbols

## The Power Symbol

BASED ON THE DIRECTION IN WHICH IT IS DEPICTED, CHO KU Rei, is used to increase or decrease power. Its objective is the light switch, revealing its capacity to light up or enlighten spiritually. Its identifying symbol is a spiral coil, which Reiki practitioners consider to be the regulator of qi. Power develops in various designs with Cho Ku Rei.

## The Distance Symbol

Hon Sha Ze Sho Nen is applied when sending qi over great distances. Its intention is timelessness, and it is commonly called Pagoda for the tower-like representation of the characters when written out. In treatments, the symbol is used to draw people together across time and space.

## The Master Symbol

Dai Ko Myo represents all that is Reiki. Its intention is wisdom and understanding. The symbol is used by Reiki masters solely when attuning initiates. It is the most complicated of the symbols to draw with the hand while performing a Reiki session.

## The Completion Symbol

The Raku symbol is used through the final stage of the Reiki attunement process. Its purpose is grounding. Practitioners apply this symbol as the Reiki treatment is drawing to a close.

## The Harmony Symbol

The Sei Hei Ki's purpose is purification. It is applied for emotional and mental healing. Practitioners may use this intention while performing treatments for depression, addiction, or anxiety to restore the body's spiritual stability. It may similarly be used to assist individuals to recover from past physical or emotional injury.

## Conclusion

Now that you have learned, witnessed, practiced, and read the proof of the effects of Reiki healing, how do you feel? Do you feel enlightened? Do you feel closer to your pets and other animals? What will you do with this information? What this book hasn't stated (until now) is that there are three levels to Reiki healing which can only be learned through taking a course and finding the right mentor to guide you through your experience. Will you take the course? Will you make Reiki a new chapter in your life? Or, will you decide what you have learned from this book and practice on your own free time with your own pets?

The choices are endless. The path is yours, and the future is unknown. Only you have the option to find your true calling in all of what you have learned and experienced. You have one life to live. Live it; share it; and believe you can achieve the impossible.

# References

Desy, P.L. (2019) Learn about the 5 Layers of Energy Surrounding Your Physical Body. Retrieved from https://www.learnreligions.com/layers-of-human-energy-field-1729677

10 Useful Applications of Reiki Healing to Improve Your Personal and Professional Life. (2017). Retrieved from https://iarp.org/ten-useful-applications-of-reiki-healing/

Reiki Distance Healing Safe Natural for Any Pet. (n.d.). Retrieved from http://animalhealings.com/reiki/

Newman, T. (2017). Everything You Need to Know About Reiki. Retrieved from https://www.medicalnewstoday.com/articles/308772.php

Healing Hands. (n.d.). Reiki For Pets. Retrieved from http://www.pethealing.net/reiki-for-pets/

Harrison, K. (2012). The Benefits of Animal Reiki. Retrieved from http://www.healinghandsnh.com/benefits-animal-reiki/

Reiki Healing For Beginners. (2019). Retrieved from https://goop.com/wellness/spirituality/reiki-for-beginners/

Reiki Energetic System. (2018). Retrieved from

https://ihreiki.com/reiki_info/reiki_energetic_system/?
v=3e8d115eb4b3

Earth Energy. (2018). Retrieved from https://ihreiki.-com/reiki_info/reiki_energetic_system/earth_energy/?
v=3e8d115eb4b3

Heavenly Energy. (2018). Retrieved from https://ihreiki.-com/reiki_info/reiki_energetic_system/heavenly_energy/?
v=3e8d115eb4b3

Heart Energy. (2018). Retrieved from https://ihreiki.-com/reiki_info/reiki_energetic_system/heart_energy/?
v=3e8d115eb4b3

Meditation 101: Techniques, Benefits, and a Beginner's How-To. (n.d.). Retrieved from
https://www.gaiam.com/blogs/discover/meditation-101-techniques-benefits-and-a-beginner-s-how-to

A Guide to the Seven Chakras and Their Meanings. (2019). Retrieved from https://www.onetribeapparel.-com/blogs/pai/seven-chakras-meaning

Reiki Meditation Shut Out The Chaos and Master Inner Peace. (2018). Retrieved from https://blog.mindvalley.-com/reiki-meditation/

Gaia, L.S. (n.d.). Reiki and Meditation. Retrieved from https://www.reiki.org/reikinews/reikimeditation.html

Everything You Need to Know About Animal Communication. (n.d.). Retrieved from https://learnhowtotalktoanimal-s.com/communication/

Paul, N.L. (n.d.). Using Reiki for the Family Pet. Retrieved from https://www.dummies.com/health/using-reiki-for-the-family-pet/

Check Her Chakras. (2017). Retrieved from
http://felinewellness.com/check-her-chakras/

Reiki for Cats: Everything You Need to Know. (2019). Retrieved from https://littlemisscat.com/reiki-for-cats-every-thing-you-need-to-know/

Gargulinski, R. (2018) Reiki For Dogs: 5 Techniques You

Can Do At Home. Retrieved from https://www.dogsnaturallymagazine.com/reiki-for-dogs-5-techniques-you-can-use-at-home/

Reiki Healing for Dogs. (n.d). Retrieved from https://caringforaseniordog.com/reiki-healing-for-dogs

Morris, C. (2015). Using Reiki for Wellness and Injury Recovery in Dogs and Other Companion Animals. Retrieved from http://www.metrodogstop.com/blog/2015/01/using-reiki-for-wellness-injury-recovery-in-dogs-and-other-companion-animals/

Prasad, K. (2017). Reiki and Canine Transitions – Kathleen Prasad's Animal Reiki Blog. Retrieved from https://www.animalreikisource.com/reiki-and-canine-transitions/

Borrowdale, L. (2017). Being a Horse Reiki Master Takes You to Some Dark Places. Retrieved from https://www.vice.com/en_nz/article/mbqz4x/being-a-horse-reiki-master-takes-you-to-some-dark-places

Reiki for Horses, The Benefits of Equine Reiki. (2018). Retrieved from https://iarp.org/reiki-for-horses-the-benefits-of-equine-reiki/

Kershaw, T. (2018). Animal Holistic Healing Case Study. Retrieved from https://www.lunacourses.com/2016/08/03/animal-holistic-healing-case-study/

Pieczurkin, J. (2016). Cleo's Reiki Transformation. Retrieved from https://shelteranimalreikiassociation.org/cleos-reiki-transformation/

Naedek, D. (2016). Reiki Meditation for Mussel and Oyster, 2 Sheltered Animals. Retrieved from https://shelteranimalreikiassociation.org/reiki-meditation-for-mussel-and-oyster-2-sheltered-animals/

Coyle, C. (2014). Reiki - Treating a Dog With Arthritis. Retrieved from https://animalwellnessguide.com/reiki-case-study-treating-a-dog-with-arthritis/

# About the Author

Monique Joiner Siedlak is a writer, witch, and warrior on a mission to awaken people to their greatest potential through the power of storytelling infused with mysticism, modern paganism, and new age spirituality. At the young age of 12, she began rigorously studying the fascinating philosophy of Wicca. By the time she was 20, she was self-initiated into the craft, and hasn't looked back ever since. To this day, she has authored over 40 books pertaining to the magick and mysteries of life.

To find out more about Monique Joiner Siedlak artistically, spiritually, and personally, feel free to visit her **official website**.

www.mojosiedlak.com

facebook.com/mojosiedlak

twitter.com/mojosiedlak

instagram.com/mojosiedlak

pinterest.com/mojosiedlak

bookbub.com/authors/monique-joiner-siedlak

# Other Books by Monique Joiner Siedlak

## Practical Magick

Wiccan Basics

Candle Magick

Wiccan Spells

Love Spells

Abundance Spells

Herb Magick

Moon Magick

Creating Your Own Spells

Gypsy Magic

## African Magic

Hoodoo

Seven African Powers: The Orishas

Cooking for the Orishas

Lucumi: The Ways of Santeria

Voodoo of Louisiana

Haitian Vodou

## The Yoga Collective

Yoga for Beginners

Yoga for Stress

Yoga for Back Pain

Yoga for Weight Loss

Yoga for Flexibility

Yoga for Advanced Beginners

Yoga for Fitness

Yoga for Runners

Yoga for Energy

Yoga for Your Sex Life

Yoga to Beat Depression and Anxiety

Yoga for Menstruation

Yoga to Detox Your Body

Yoga to Tone Your Body

## A Natural Beautiful You

Creating Your Own Body Butter

Creating Your Own Body Scrub

Creating Your Own Body Spray

# Last Chance
# Join My Newsletter!

If you missed it, I have a free gift available for you and wanted to remind you it's still available.

mojosiedlak.com/self-help-and-yoga-newsletter

Thank you for reading my book.
I really appreciate all your feedback and would love to hear what you have to say! Please leave your review at your favorite retailer!

*Thank you*

www.ingramcontent.com/pod-product-compliance
Lightning Source LLC
Chambersburg PA
CBHW071607040426
42452CB00008B/1265